The Politics of TESOL Education

The Politics of TESOL Education

Writing, Knowledge, Critical Pedagogy

Vai Ramanathan

RoutledgeFalmer
Taylor & Francis Group

NEW YORK AND LONDON

Published in 2002 by
RoutledgeFalmer
29 West 35th Street
New York, New York 10001
www.routledge-ny.com

Published in Great Britain by
RoutledgeFalmer
11 New Fetter Lane
London EC4P 4EE
www.routledgefalmer.com

RoutledgeFalmer is an imprint of the Taylor & Francis Group.

A version of chapter 1 appeared as Ramanathan, V., Davies, C. E., and Schleppegrell, M. (2001). A naturalistic inquiry into the cultures of two divergent MA-TEOL programs: Implications for TESOL. *TESOL Quarterly* 35(2), 279–305.

Portions of chapters 1 and 5 appeared as Ramanathan, V. (2002). Enhancing the critical edge of (L2) teacher education: Some issues in advanced literacy. In M. Schleppegrell and C. Colombi (Eds.), *Developing Advanced Literacy: Meaning with Power* (pp. 187–207). Mahwah, NJ: Lawrence Erlbaum Associates. Reprinted by permission.

An earlier version of chapter 3 appeared as Ramanathan, V., and Kaplan, R. B. (2000). Genres, authors, discourse communities: Theory and application for L1 and L2 writing instructors. *Journal of Second Language Writing* 9(2), 171–191. Reprinted by permission of Elsevier Science.

A portion of chapter 4 appeared as Ramanathan, V. (2000). Some problematic channels in the teaching and critical thinking in current composition textbooks: Implications for L2 student writers. *Issues in Applied Linguistics* 7(2), 225–249. Reprinted by permission.

A portion of chapter 4 appeared as Ramanathan, V., and Kaplan, R. B. (1996). Audience and voice in current L1 composition texts: Some implications for ESL student writers. *Journal of Second Language Writing* 5(1), 21–34. Reprinted by permission of Elsevier Science.

10 9 8 7 6 5 4 3 2 1

Library of Congress Cataloging-in-Publication Data
  Ramanthan, Vai.
The politics of TESOL education : writing, knowledge, critical pedagogy /
Vai Ramanathan.
p.   cm.
Includes bibliographical references (p.) and index.
ISBN 0-415-93352-8—ISBN 0-415-93353-6 (pbk.)
1. English language—Study and teaching—Foreign speakers. 2. English language—Study and teaching—Foreign speakers—Political aspects. 3. Report writing——Study and teaching—Political aspects. I. Title.
PE 1128.A2R25 2002
428'.0071—dc21   2002017898

Contents

Acknowledgments

This book, as with all books, has emerged from a range of events and contexts and does not by any means mark the end of a process for me. At best an artificial break in my researching endeavors, it will be read, I hope, as a text that recognizes the fluidity of the researching enterprise and the selective nature and orientation of all research agendas, including the crucial one of English-language teaching and learning (ELTL). The take on ELTL that I present here is not only one of many but represents where I currently am as an educator and researcher, and it is likely to evolve and change as I continue in the field.

Far too many circumstances have influenced this book for me to enumerate: my upbringing and educational/research experiences in India (which partially inform my cross-cultural stance), my years as a teaching assistant in freshman composition at University of Southern California (which have influenced my takes on writing-related issues), the different universities and teacher education programs with which I have been affiliated (which have opened my eyes to the divergent nature of this enterprise). As for the people who have influenced my thinking, they also are too numerous to list. There are scores of researchers whose works I have read and been stimulated by, but whom I have not had the good fortune to meet or to know personally. I mentally include them in the thanks I offer here.

Some professional and personal relationships, however, do stand out. Paul Johnson's editorial suggestions and Mary Dorian's copyediting have made this book that much more readable. My friends Catherine Davies and Mary Schleppegrell not only gave me kind permission to integrate our collective research in this book but remain the best friends possible. Jody Abbott, Suguna Ramanathan, James Gee, and Suresh Canagarajah gave me invaluable advice and feedback on chapters-in-progress. Fragments of conversations I have had with Dwight Atkinson, Sarah Benesch, Salli Davis, Dana Ferris,

John Hedgcock, Eli Hinkel, Ann Johns, Jim Raymond, and George Wolfe have by various means made their way into this book. My family, the Abbott and Ramanathan clans—with six-year-old Aasha straddling them both—stand, as always, firmly behind me.

As for the two sterling men to whom this book is dedicated, I will not gild the lily by saying too much: The first unreservedly stretches a hand to pull me up; the second remains the other silent author of this writing. Both men know what and how much I owe them.

For Jody,
for bailing me out,
and
For Robert B. Kaplan,
a thousand salaams now

Politicizing MA-TESOL and L2 Teacher Education

Whenever one can describe, between a number of statements, such a system of dispersion, whenever, between objects, types of statement, concepts, or thematic choices, one can define a regularity (an order, correlations, positions and functionings, transformations), we will say, for the sake of convenience, that we are dealing with a discursive formation. . . . The conditions to which the elements of this division (objects, mode of statement, concepts, thematic choices) are subjected we shall call the rules of formation. The rules of formation are the conditions of existence (but also of coexistence, maintenance, modification and disappearance) in a given discursive formation.

—Michel Foucault, *The Archaeology of Knowledge*

Primarily concerned with how power operates at various levels of schooling, researchers in critical pedagogy and critical language awareness (Fairclough, 1992) have demonstrated particular interest in issues related to the "political economy of schooling, the state and education, the representation of texts, and the construction of student subjectivity" (McLaren, 1989, p. 159). Although critical pedagogists have varied in their points of focus,[1] with interests ranging from the libertarian to the radical and the liberationist, they seem largely allied in their commitment to certain objectives, namely to empower the powerless and to find ways of addressing and transforming social inequalities in the schooling world. Research in this domain has been both theoretical and practical, with theorists privileging ways of conceptualizing schooling, education, and self-awareness (Aronowitz and Giroux,

1993) and practitioners preferring critical ethnographical strategies (e.g., Canagarajah, 1993).

The Politics of TESOL Education focuses on an area of critical pedagogy that has been referred to as "advanced literacy" (Schleppegrell and Colombi, 2002). Specifically, I examine the theoretical and practical issues attending the development of L1 and L2 teachers in training. Impossible as it is to arrive at one concise definition of *advanced literacy*—given that different researchers use the phrase in different ways and in different contexts—I use it to mean two things: (1) the measure of what people do with reading and writing at tertiary levels of schooling and beyond, and (2) the measure of a person's ability to question and critique the different disciplinary components into which L1 and L2 teachers are socialized as they go through their professional training. My purpose is to empower these teachers to transform their worlds by encouraging in them a meta-awareness— a heightened awareness of how their thinking evolves as they are being socialized into their disciplines. (Thus, the notions of advanced literacy, critical pedagogy, and meta-awareness are all inextricably linked.)

Although a degree of meta-awareness is assumed in the general process of empowerment (you cannot, after all, address problems in your existing condition unless you have reflected on them and recognized your own participation in this condition), meta-awareness in itself has not been fully developed as a distinct mode of operation in the general area of L2 teacher education. Encouraging future teachers to engage in critical reflection, questioning, and analysis of the various facets that make up their TESOL/applied linguistics worlds—the immediate programs in which they are enrolled and the larger discipline(s) into which they are being inducted—is a first step in this direction. Encouraging teachers-in-training to address and analyze some of the very facets that constitute their programs and the larger discipline(s) will empower them to start thinking in terms of how they can, collectively and as individuals, effect changes they believe necessary. I use Fleck's notion of "thought collectives" (hereafter TCs; Fleck, 1981) to refer to the individual programs and discipline(s) of these teachers-in-training, and the following pages offer a definition of the phrase. An in-depth discussion of TCs in general is offered in chapter 1.

Critical Pedagogy, Teacher Education, and TESOL: Where and How This Study Is Positioned

Recent research in critical pedagogy has focused partially on ways to rethink the role of the teacher. Giroux (1992) maintains that educators at all levels of schooling need to be seen as "intellectuals . . . who, as mediators, legitimators, and producers of ideas and social practices, perform a pedagogical function that is eminently political in nature" (p. 31). Viewing and constructing teachers as intellectuals would be empowering in that we would see them as individuals who have the courage to question authority and who refuse to act counter to their experience or judgment. Such teachers would be more likely to try out "parallel pedagogies" (Shor and Freire, 1987, p. 44), alongside the conventional teaching practices they are expected to follow, toward liberating themselves and their students from traditional, restrictive schooling protocols. They would be able to make the pedagogical political and vice versa—a feature that Giroux (1992) maintains ultimately makes for new forms of culture, alternative social practices, new modes of communication, and a practical vision for the future.

Research in teacher education—especially in L2 studies—has not been particularly critical, however. Issues vary across a range of domains, from reconceptualizing current teacher training programs (Freeman and Johnson, 1998), to having potential teachers trace their evolution through diary entries they keep (Bailey and Nunan, 1996), to encouraging reflective practice (Nunan, 1992; Richards and Lockhart, 1994), to advocating "dialogic inquiry" (Schleppegrell, 1997) so that teachers develop a richer knowledge base about their students' backgrounds, motivations, and learning strategies.

Focus, on the whole, has tended to be on areas such as modifying current TESOL programs and reevaluating the position and role of the potential teacher in the ESL classroom. Except for Hedgcock (2002) little or no attention has been paid to making teachers criti-

cally aware of how they contribute to maintaining the discursive practices and culture of their discipline even as they are being socialized
by the culture themselves. Although Freeman and Johnson (1998)
advocate a more central role for the teacher in the teaching-learning
exchange—in which the teacher's prior knowledge, rationalizations,
decisions, immediate contexts, and the schooling environments are
all recognized as crucial components of a teacher education program—they do not take into consideration larger disciplinary
sociopolitical practices that shape the teacher. Freeman and
Johnson's overall case for rethinking current TESOL programs may
be a good one, especially given that many programs overemphasize
"discrete amounts of knowledge usually in the form of theories and
methods" (p. 399); however, the kind of focus they advocate for the
"activity of teaching"—scrutinizing the teacher who "does it" and "the
contexts and pedagogy by which it is carried out" (p. 397)—does not
encourage teachers to contextualize their position in terms of the politics of the discipline. Thus, although Freeman (1996) finds that the
"local language [of enrolled teachers] becomes more critical as they
cast their experiences in terms of discourse they are being socialized
into," this "local language" does not reflect meta-awareness of disciplinary concerns: how as TESOLers they sustain and reproduce
certain valued genres and text types in the discipline, how their cognitions are shaped by what is immediately available in their environments, how materials they use in classrooms are not as value free as
they seem.[2]

Richards and Lockhart (1994) also advocate reflective practices,
encouraging teachers to examine their teaching goals, for instance,
but they do not encourage critical reflection and questioning in
terms of the teacher's role vis-à-vis various aspects of the discipline.
It is precisely this gap that my writing attempts to bridge. I draw my
examples from the applied linguistics/TESOL communities because
I know these communities best. I do believe, however, that my discussions of particular facets of the teaching-learning enterprise are
relevant to all L1 and L2 potential teachers. Specific details regarding
the primary and secondary audiences for this book follow.

Meta-Awareness and Thought Collectives: Definitions and Expansions

Ludwig Fleck (1981), from whom I have borrowed the term *thought collective*, defines it as follows:

> A thought collective exists wherever two or more people are actually exchanging thoughts. He is a poor observer who does not notice that a stimulating conversation between two persons soon creates a condition in which each utters thoughts he would not have been able to produce either by himself or in different company. A special mood arises, which would not otherwise affect either partner of the conversation but almost always returns whenever these persons meet again. Prolonged duration of this state, produces, from common understanding and mutual misunderstanding, a thought structure [Denkgebilde] that belongs to neither of them alone but nevertheless is not at all without meaning. Who is its carrier and who its originator? It is neither more nor less than the collective of [two] persons. If a third person joins in, a new collective arises. The previous mood will dissolve and with it the special creative force of the former [small] collective. (p. 44)

Fleck's thought collectives are relatively small and transient, involving only two people. I use the term, however, in a somewhat more expansive sense, to refer to a *relatively stable disciplinary community*. Implied in Fleck's quote is the idea that a thought collective holds people with shared interests, goals, ideas, and events together with visible and invisible ties. It is easy to see, for instance, how two TESOLers, who may be complete strangers to each other, can connect (at a TESOL conference, for example) because of a thought structure shared among members of the discipline. This sharing can occur because of numerous connections within the TC, including relations linking researchers, teachers, genres, texts, teaching practices, events, activities, lectures, hallway chats, and student conferences. Prolonged duration of such sharing thus "produces, from common understanding and mutual misunderstanding, a thought structure" that belongs to the collective. Having potential teachers identify, reflect on, and question the various components that make up their thought collectives, as well as their own individual contribution toward the stability of these components, will afford them a critical and multidimensional view that is otherwise not possible. Such self-conscious critical reflection on the very components in which they are engaged and into which they are being socialized will ultimately heighten their meta-awareness.

My suggestions for ways that such meta-awareness can be achieved are intended to contribute to and promote debate about issues in teacher education. I do not claim to provide definitive solutions here. I do suggest, however, that although I may at times appear to take a theoretical bent, the suggestions I present (especially in chapter 6) are practical ways that teacher education programs can build a critical edge into all areas of individual programs. Such an approach is in keeping with the idea that turning the critical lens on ourselves allows us to engage in "reflexive researching" (Ramanathan, 1997)—an endeavor that attempts to uncloak social practices that "mask many difficult and misleading assumptions about the purpose and politics of our work" (Myers, 1988, p. 622). Thus, it is not enough that we have our (L2) teachers-in-training become literate by "picking up the tools of the trade." They must be able to talk critically about what is involved in picking up these tools as they engage in the process of doing so (Blanton, 1998; Heath, 1985).

Such awareness will enhance the professional astuteness of teachers-in-training, encouraging them to question their practices, regardless of the contexts within which they find themselves (including EFL vs. ESL cultural contexts, community colleges, K–12 settings, intensive English programs, composition programs, refugee institutions). Clearly such meta-awareness cannot be gauged by conventional numerical measures of assessment without running the risk of seeming arbitrary and imposed. Notional and fuzzy, this concept is perhaps best addressed in terms of how teachers can be encouraged to make the kind of professional judgments that Dewey recognized as "the relative indicative or signifying values of the various features of the perplexing situation; to know what to let go of as of no account; what to eliminate as irrelevant; what to retain as conducive to the outcome; what to emphasize as a clew to the difficulty. This power in ordinary matters we call *knack, tact, cleverness*; in more important affairs, *insight, discernment*" (quoted in Simpson and Jackson, 1997, p. 198, Dewey's emphasis). Among teachers, the development of such judgments is believed to partially grow with articulated reflection on individual teaching practices,[3] and within the realm of TESOL, for instance, this point, as mentioned earlier, has been developed and made accessible by Richards and Lockhart (1996).

Although I agree with Richards and Lockhart's idea that teachers contemplate their practices, beliefs, and assumptions,[4] I want to go a step further by encouraging teachers to critically meditate on and question two issues mentioned previously: (1) *the discipline's social practices* and (2) *their individual participation in these practices*. This process includes encouraging L2 teachers to frequently reflect on, address, and question their teaching goals in relation to larger disciplinary concerns: for example, ways that genres operate in various realms of their disciplines, how their professional goals are tied to the goals of the discipline(s), how debates in the discipline(s) percolate down to the smaller contexts of their individual classrooms, how they contribute to text types and genres remaining stable or changing in their disciplines, and how "basic facts" and "truths" in their disciplines can, from another point of view, be regarded as highly questionable.

Heightening teachers' overall meta-awareness to where they begin talking and thinking about how their TCs function and are sustained, and how as teachers they individually contribute to the overall functioning and sustenance of TCs, is crucial because only when student teachers are aware of issues and problems in their TCs can they begin to effect changes. One way of heightening this awareness is by making teachers conscious—*through active reflection and questioning*—of how their programs and discipline(s) function as activity systems with cognitions distributed across various components (which I will examine in depth in chapter 1). It is in this sense that I advocate a defamiliarizing stance toward everything in our professional realm, including genres, textbooks, and curricular materials, to afford us one way of being critical. Distancing ourselves—however artificially and temporarily—from the professional facets we are engaged in allows us, if only in fleeting moments, to discern our role in the construction of our present circumstances. Once we are able to see ourselves and our local worlds from a different perspective, we will be in a better position to envision changes.

Key Issues

Before I turn to the key questions motivating my writing, I want to clarify my intended audience. This book should be relevant to all professionals involved in English-language teaching and learning (ELTL) and L1 teachers. Because of my disciplinary background and orientation as an applied sociolinguist, however, some of the issues will resonate most strongly with L2 educators and TESOLers enrolled in MA and PhD programs, especially those being trained to teach college-bound, tertiary-level, ESL undergraduate students (in community colleges, intensive language institutes, and four-year universities). I have also oriented the book toward issues related to the teaching and learning of writing for several reasons: (1) writing is a language "skill" that many graduating TESOLers are expected to teach in tertiary institutions; (2) student aptitude/proficiency for L1 and L2 students in content and language areas is (at least in the humanities and social sciences) typically assessed in terms of written performance; (3) knowledge in applied linguistics/TESOL is to a large extent constructed by and through writing; and (4) having taught L1 and L2 writing and writing instructors for several years, I am invested in this area and am thus comfortable speaking about it. Although I do not by any means aim to devalue other language skills by ostensibly promoting writing, I do believe that writing (and reading) is accorded importance at the tertiary level in ways that speaking and listening are not.

I raise at least three central issues, none of which have been adequately addressed either as researchable areas in themselves or as domains pertinent to (L2) teacher education. Capturing facets in the TESOL/applied linguistics TCs that demand critical reflection and questioning, these issues address disciplinary components such as teaching materials, genres, and text types and disciplinary social practices, all of which come down to those of us in the profession as the kind of official knowledge we need to know in order to be considered full participants in the TCs. I will argue that it is precisely the *discursive formation* of disciplinary facets being aligned in particular ways that calls for questioning and scrutiny because the "rules of formation" (Foucault, 1972) are not as neutral and value-free as they seem. The following issues I discuss relate to concerns regarding the discipline at large and to smaller components within the discipline.

Questioning the profession's practices: ways in which practices in individual, local TESOL programs reflect issues in the larger discipline. An area not adequately addressed in TESOL or L2 teacher education is making potential teachers aware of how their current cognitions are shaped by factors in their immediate environments (the small TC, namely the programs they are enrolled in) and by factors in the larger discipline. Because of departmental and community constraints, certain MA-TESOL programs emphasize particular L2 teaching skills over others (Ramanathan, Davies, and Schleppegrell, 2001). Drawing on an in-depth discussion of two divergent MA-TESOL programs in different parts of the United States, I will call attention to ways in which L2 student teachers get trained in vastly different teaching skills. The extended, naturalistic study of the cultures of the two programs will argue that the programs' respective identities are markedly shaped by local, departmental, campus-wide, and community constraints. The two programs are housed in two different departments—one in English, the other in linguistics—and to stay viable, each has little choice but to assume the ideological underpinnings of its larger department. As the analysis reveals, L2 student teachers from the English department gain most of their practical experience teaching skills of composition/writing to ESL students, whereas those in linguistics gain more experience teaching skills of speaking and listening.

The potential TESOLers in the two programs thus have their current "knowledges"—cognitions, skills, and expertise—shaped by local conditions. Heightening awareness among L2 teachers of such divergence in MA-TESOL programs will enable them to ask the next set of critical questions: What does such divergence in L2 teacher education mean for the TESOL discipline? Do we need to collectively rethink current TESOL standards? Does TESOL need to come up with criteria directly targeting ESL students at tertiary levels (current criteria seem applicable only to K–12 students)? Encouraging TESOLers to reflect on and question the discipline's practices and norms in terms of their locally evolving professional identities is crucial if we want them to become critically astute teachers; only through such reflection will they be able to effect necessary changes in the discipline.

Questioning how genres and text types socialize TESOLers into particular disciplinary practices and the importance of empowering TESOLers to recognize that they can shape their TCs by changing sociotextual conventions should they feel they need to. Although there has been plenty of research on genres and the ways they function in particular disciplines (Atkinson, 1998b), there has been little or no attention paid to addressing ways that critical genre awareness might be cultivated in potential L2 teachers as a way of heightening their meta-awareness. The last decade has produced significant research on the sociocognitive nature of genre evolution. Berkenkotter and Huckin (1993), for example, focus on how "knowledge production [in the different disciplines] is carried out and codified largely through generic forms of writing: lab reports, working papers, reviews, grant proposals, technical reports, conference papers, journal articles, monographs and so forth" (p. 476). Genre researchers such as Swales (1990) and Miller (1984) maintain that through recurrent use these conventionalized forms of writing become vehicles by which knowledge and information get disseminated to a community of people with shared interests. As researchers and educators in the applied linguistics/TESOL communities, we all contribute to the rigidifying of particular writing conventions by gauging student and peer performance partially on the extent to which that performance conforms to our (written) discourse expectations (Ramanathan-Abbott, 1993)—that is, we ensure that particular disciplinary genres maintain some modicum of inherent stability.[5]

On a macro level, however, genres are also dynamic and likely to change depending on the evolving sociocognitive needs of discourse communities. The essay that the average freshman composition student has to write, for instance, bears little resemblance to its eighteenth-century forebear. Teachers have a responsibility to sensitize potential TESOLers (especially writing instructors) to some ways in which they—partially in their participation in certain disciplinary social practices and their respective evolutions as "authors"—contribute to the general (in)flexibility of genres. Heightening their genre awareness will contribute to their overall metaknowledge, making them conscious of their pedagogical practices and increasing their awareness of their position in macro-level genre disciplinary processes.

Such language awareness is crucial because "not only is education itself a key domain of linguistically mediated power, [but] it also mediates other key domains for learners, including the adult world of work" (Fairclough, 1995, p. 217). Social and textual practices that all of us—instructors, researchers, teachers—draw on without thinking embody assumptions that directly or indirectly legitimize the status quo, and conventions that are seemingly ordinary, usual, or commonsensical seem that way because they have become naturalized. Making (L2) instructors conscious of the various social practices that contribute to genre stability and genre change, and how their participation in particular disciplinary activities contributes to these forces, will allow them to locate themselves in a multidimensional constellation of sociotextual practices.[6] Such awareness will have lasting, positive consequences in the discipline: it will ultimately enable teachers to question, address, and (re)shape disciplinary (sociotextual) practices that they may find problematic and needy of a response.

Questioning what is appropriate written knowledge—specifically college-level academic prose—and how this knowledge is to be displayed and the (textual) politics of such display. Displaying knowledge in writing is particularly problematic for L2 students because they may not have had opportunities to acquire the necessary North American sociotextual conventions of how to appropriately present what they know. L2 students often have to acquire a new (and narrow) set of display conventions from/in their writing classes that are influenced and shaped by a range of factors in both TCs and the larger culture and that, as such, beg for uncovering and scrutiny. Encouraging potential L2 teachers to critically question and analyze, among other things, the sociotextual and cultural assumptions in what they emphasize and how they teach, as well as what they expect from ESL students in terms of written products, is crucial to enhancing a degree of relativity in these teachers-in-training.

In general, there has been little scholarship calling for potential L2 teachers to uncover aspects of the official knowledge regarding writing instruction, and it is important that potential TESOLers be encouraged to look for and analyze problematic assumptions in the L2 writing materials they use or review, including textbooks and the jargon in them, as well as the modes by which these texts impart writing skills. Uncovering latent assumptions in frequently used rhetorical terms in these textbooks—such as *audience, voice,* and *critical thinking*—I will show by example one way of unpacking these value-laden terms. L2 writing materials in general—and textbooks in particular—draw on a shared pool of sociocognitive practices that mainstream students have access to but L2 students very often do not share. This point is important given that many L2 writing materials are drawn from the L1 world and are often used without appropriate consideration of the underlying linguistic complexities in the L2 classroom. Based on a survey of L1 writing textbooks frequently used in L2 classrooms, this book will highlight the need for potential TESOLers to adopt a critical stance toward given disciplinary terms. Such critical examination and questioning opens up the possibility of viewing pedagogic materials—including the writing processes and textual forms they encourage—as embedded in a complex nexus of textual, political, and cultural rules of discursive formation. It also allows us to challenge particular ideologies promoted by writing materials—*the* writing process, for instance—as being dynamic and plural.

The sociopolitical and cultural stances promoted in the following chapters represent a select set of possibilities that could be taken regarding disciplinary facets. As will become apparent, it is important that TESOLers become aware of how their knowledge of practices in the TCs is partially shaped, for example, not only by disciplinary facets such as textbooks produced en masse and driven by the commercial needs of publishing houses but by interpretations they read about the generation and use of these texts. All three of the previously mentioned issues embody various aspects of the profession's official knowledge. This knowledge, however—what gets included and excluded—signifies complex political, social, historical, and cultural forces and rifts, so what eventually emerges and gets sanctified as official knowledge is often the result of a complex set of negotiations between a range of local factors in small and large TCs. Amid the negotiations, though, is evidence of ways that the values of one (dominant) cultural group win out over others. Textbooks, curricular materials, pedagogic practices, and program orientations are examples of this selectivity. As Apple and Christian-Smith (1991) point out, such selectivity signifies "particular constructions of reality, particular ways of selecting and organizing that vast universe of possible knowledge . . . someone's selection, someone's vision of legitimate knowledge and culture, one that in the process of enfranchising one group's cultural capital disenfranchises another's" (pp. 3–4). Encouraging potential (L2) teachers to recognize how local issues in classrooms are embedded in social practices and how, as participants, teachers contribute to sustaining and reproducing these practices will foster initial steps toward addressing issues of inequality. It will heighten awareness of the importance of peeling away some sociocultural, textual, and historical politics regarding our curricular and pedagogic theories and practices. Such an endeavor should enable all of us as ESL professionals to "place our institutions of formal education back into the larger unequal society of which they are a part" (Apple, 1990, p. ix) and to take constructive steps in addressing issues that call for change.

Conclusion and Chapter Breakdown

It could be argued that it makes no difference, as far as language teaching goes, to have our potential teachers become meta-aware; after all, they will gain a degree of meta-awareness as they stay on and participate in the field. On the one hand, the kind of meta-awareness they will garner from simply being immersed in the field will not necessarily equip them with a set of critical skills that will empower them to respond to disciplinary issues that need change. On the other hand, making them meta-aware of their socialization process into their TCs will not only empower them to respond to program- and discipline-wide concerns in appropriate ways, but it will give them a fuller sense of how individual programs and the larger profession function and of their respective places in these TCs. This awareness is crucial if we want our TESOLers to make reflective and judicious judgments about facets in their TCs—including teaching materials, genres, and their own evolving cognitions—because these judgments have direct consequences not only in the classroom but in the field at large.

There is another reason for facilitating such understanding. Materials regarding language teacher education—where the nuts and bolts of the job are learned—have typically tended to concentrate on classroom performance, with some theory on the side. "Information about teaching has generally been normative rather than descriptive, and when descriptive then based on categories external to the situation and to the participants" (Woods, 1996, p. 21). Research in TESOL has not yet advocated the need for a critical edge to be built into the discipline. Heightening this critical awareness and the general importance of doing so is what this book is about. Explicating the notion of TCs by relating it to already existing, relevant theories, chapter 1 addresses ways in which cultures and knowledges of TCs are formed, sustained, aligned, and sometimes changed, as well as the general importance of heightening meta-awareness of such issues.

Moving into the more specific domain of individual teacher education programs, chapter 2 examines the local contexts of two divergent MA-TESOL programs in different parts of the United States. This chapter is an attempt to raise consciousness about how and why particular MA-TESOL programs stress certain language teaching skills and the general implications and consequences of graduating L2 teachers socialized in divergent programs on the larger field of TESOL. By encouraging reflection and questioning of some ways that the individual identities of MA-TESOL programs depend on factors in their respective local environments (which in turn shape the teaching skills with which enrolled L2 teachers graduate), the chapter demonstrates by example ways in which the divergent evolving cognitions of TESOLers are, to a large extent, shaped by the programs in which they are enrolled.

Chapter 3 examines genres and the ways that certain social practices render text types stable, whereas other practices propel them into gradual change. Charting out some ways that particular genres in TESOL/applied linguistics and other disciplines manifest such tendencies, this chapter details how sociotextual conventions in TCs function, and it underscores the need to make potential L2 teachers meta-aware of how they contribute to genre stability and to genre change through participation in their TCs. Making potential L2 teachers reflect on their location vis-à-vis particular sociotextual norms and conventions, as well as making them metacognitively aware of their gradual mastery over particular forms—a mastery that emerges as much from their teaching of certain forms as from using these forms themselves—will enable them to take critical stances toward themselves as teachers and researchers.

Moving into still more specific domains, chapter 4 addresses textbooks. Specifically, it wrestles with issues related to how written knowledge is best displayed and the generally implicit norms by which writing is taught and presented in tertiary-level writing textbooks. It underscores, among other things, latent sociocultural assumptions advocated in the stances held in these texts. Revisiting some dominant strains, chapter 5 offers practical suggestions for building meta-awareness into our current teacher education programs. Reinforcing this book's dominant theme, this chapter asserts, among other things, the central premise on which the current argument is based—namely, it is not enough that (L2) student teachers pick up the tools of the trade; rather, all of us should be able to talk critically about what is involved in picking up these tools as we are in the process of doing so. As Gee has said, "Meta-knowledge is power, because it leads to the ability to manipulate, to analyze, to resist, while advancing. Such meta-knowledge can eventually make 'maladapted' students smarter than 'adapted' ones" (1990, pp. 148–149).

Chapter 1

The Politics of (TESOL) Thought Collectives

> *One could say that the sociological understanding of "reality" and "knowledge" falls somewhere in the middle between that of the man in the street and that of the philosopher. The man in the street does not ordinarily trouble himself about what is "real" to him and about what he "knows" unless he is stopped short by some sort of problem. He takes his "reality" and his "knowledge" for granted. The sociologist cannot do this, if only because of his systematic awareness of the fact that men in the street take quite different "realities" for granted as between one society and another. The sociologist is forced by the very logic of his discipline to ask, if nothing else, whether the difference between the two "realities" may not be understood in relation to various differences between the two societies. The philosopher, on the other hand, is professionally obligated to take nothing for granted, and to obtain maximal clarity as to the ultimate status of what the man in the street believes to be "reality" and "knowledge."*
> —Berger and Luckmann, *The Social Construction of Reality*

What we take to be reality is partially constructed by what is physically, mentally, emotionally, and materially accessible to us. Although philosophical debates of what reality is may be generally irrelevant to, say, a farmer, it is conceived of differently by sociologists and philosophers, using divergent disciplinary lenses and asking very different kinds of questions. Each of us in academia (and everywhere else) has numerous realities (being a linguist, parent, spouse, daughter) with degrees of difference and overlap among them. Identifying and questioning aspects of

TESOL-related realities—how they shape us and how we in turn shape them—is the subject of this chapter.

One way to gauge the relative parameters of our realities is through a process of elimination because specifying what our realities are not affords them some definition. Another way of gauging our realties is by seeing ways in which they connect to other realities. Identifying related territories and areas of overlap complexifies our realities by adding to them dimensions that the process of elimination does not. This chapter attempts to engage in both kinds of TESOL realities identification in relation to the notion of TCs. Although this may appear to be a roundabout way to define a term, the process is deliberate.

Because the notion of TCs is fuzzy, it can best be explained by its (lack of) connections to other (related) terms. First, by engaging in a process of elimination, I attempt to discern what TCs are not by specifying how they differ from related terms such as *discourse communities* (Swales, 1990, 1998) and *discourses* (Gee, 1990). Next, in a process of expansion, I explain how various theories, including those related to the sociology of knowledge and activity systems, inform the current discussion of how knowledge production in the TCs is situated, aligned, and distributed. Engaging in both kinds of definition allows me to show TCs as somewhat autonomous, free-floating entities that, although moored to "real" worlds, constitute worlds of their own—worlds that play a crucial role in shaping the professional cognitions of currently engaged L2 teachers, researchers, and scholars.

TCs, Discourse Communities, and Discourses

Two terms that overlap with TCs are *discourse communities* and *discourses*, and in this section I would like to establish how TCs differ from them. The differences, as we will see, have to do with varying points of focus.

The term *discourse community* has been much debated in the last decade (Berkenkotter and Huckin, 1993; Ramanathan and Kaplan, 2000; Swales, 1998). Although I do not aim to offer a comprehensive review of previous explanations of this term (see Swales, 1998, for a relatively full review), I would like to briefly mention some key definitions because these are subsumed in the general understanding of TCs as presented in this book. Each of the following definitions centers on a different focal point.

A discourse community with a focus on texts. James Porter (1992), who offers a poststructuralist definition, maintains that "the term discourse community is useful for describing a space that was unacknowledged. . . . What was before largely scene, unnoticed background, becomes foreground" (p. 84). He explains:

> A discourse community is a local and temporary constraining system, *defined by a body of texts* [my emphasis] (or more generally, practices) that are unified by a common focus. A discourse community is a *textual system* [my emphasis] with stated and unstated conventions, a vital history, mechanisms for wielding power, institutional hierarchies, vested interests, and so on. Thus, a *discourse* [original emphasis] community cuts across sociological or institutional boundaries. (p. 106)

Among the advantages that Porter mentions is the fact that this term focuses directly on "texts in terms of rhetorical principles of operation (and is thus closely allied to rhetoric as a discipline)" (p. 88).[1] Texts—their composition, reproduction, and dissemination—are thus key points of emphasis in Porter's interpretation of discourse communities.

A discourse community with a focus on groups. Moving away from texts as a central feature, Killingsworth and Gilbertson (1992) stress groups of readers and writers as constituting discourse communities. They distinguish between *local* and *global* discourse communities. Groups of readers and writers in the former typically "work together in companies, colleges, departments, neighborhoods, government agencies or other groups defined by specific demographic features," whereas those in the latter are defined exclusively by a commitment to particular kinds of action and discourse, regardless of where and with whom they work (1992, p. 162). Killingsworth and Gilbertson fine-tune their definition with other distinctions: that "local communities . . . may monitor membership by physical surveillance (corporate badges, parking stickers, correct dress . . .)," whereas "membership in global communities tends to be regulated exclusively by discourse-governed criteria (writing style, publication in certain journals . . .)" (1992, p. 169). As Swales (1998) points out, the two types of discourse communities can often come into conflict "as they compete for the loyalties of individual members of both" (p. 201).

A discourse community with a focus on place. The idea of place discourse communities (Swales, 1998) appears to be closely tied to "communities of practice" (Lave and Wenger, 1991) in that it orients the term around a "project site" (Swales, 1998): "A community of practice is an aggregate of people who come together around mutual engagement in an endeavor. Ways of doing things, ways of talking, beliefs, values, power relations—in short, practices—emerge in the course of this mutual endeavor" (Eckert and McConnell-Ginet, 1992, p. 464, quoted in Swales, 1998, p. 202). The idea that a site/place is its own community recalls Lave and Wenger's (1991) notion of *legitimate peripheral participation,* which they believe addresses the issue of how newcomers to a group get initiated into the group's practices (I address this in some detail in the next section). Learners inevitably participate in communities of practitioners, and "the mastery of knowledge and skill requires newcomers to move toward full participation in the socio-cultural practice of a community" (1991, p. 29).

I turn now to how thought collectives differ from discourse communities. The key difference appears to be focus. The notion of thought collectives *centers on the (development of) thoughts and professional cognitions of people who participate in them,* so texts, sites, and groups are seen to primarily emerge from collective cognitions. None of the previously mentioned definitions of *discourse community* focus on the development of thoughts and cog-

nitions of participants. Although such sociocognitive development may be implied in these various definitions, it is made
explicit in this book through the term *thought collectives*.

TCs also overlap with Gee's notion of a discourse, which he
defines as "a socially accepted association among ways of using
language, of thinking, feeling, believing, valuing, and of acting
that can be used to identify oneself as a member of a socially
meaningful group or 'social network,' or to signal (that one is
playing) a socially meaningful 'role'" (1990, p. 143). Gee sees *discourse* as an all-encompassing term, the individual's "'identity-
kit,' which comes complete with the appropriate costume and
instructions on how to act, talk, and often write so as to take on a
particular social role that others will recognize" (Gee, 1990,
p. 142). Gee focuses on the entire individual to address how all of
the various subdiscourses make up his or her being. The notion
of TCs, in contrast, with its focus on the collective cognitions of
participants in a community, isolates the sociocognitive realm for
closer examination. As with the term *discourse community*, the difference between discourse and thought collective is one of focus.

Defining TCs by Expansion: Socially Constructing Knowledge in TCs

Having established how TCs differ from related terms, I address
the notion in relation to other theories. If TCs are partially formed
and sustained by social practices and norms, then it follows that
knowledge within those collectives is socially constructed as well.
The question of what it means to know something is more complex than it seems. As humans we do not just observe, look, see,
and formulate. How we see, what we see, what lenses we wear
when seeing, what we take in and why, how we put together what
we see and know in ways that make sense to us (and others) are
shaped by a range of social elements that make up our sociocognitive maps. Ways of thinking and knowing seem to reveal
more about the collective practices of groups of people than
they do about individual thinkers (McCarthy, 1996). Indeed, as

Durkheim (1915) believed, the collective bases of our ideas render a uniformity and impersonality to our thoughts (where impersonal reason becomes another name given to collective thought). As McCarthy (1996) points out, when we reason or argue, we draw on concepts attributable more to shared or impersonal sources, whose qualities are always general and permanent, than to particular individuals. Collective ideas, that is, have a quality of impersonal rationality, what Anderson (1991) calls a "halo of disinterestedness."

Two related propositions (McCarthy, 1996) are relevant to this discussion of collective knowledge production. The first is that *knowledge is socially determined* (Mannheim, 1952). All human thought has social origins because human consciousness is embedded in real life—that is, actual social conditions shared by particular collectives. The second proposition maintains that "knowledges are not merely the outcome of a social order but are themselves key forces in the creation and communication of a social order" (McCarthy, 1996, p. 12). We might even say that *knowledge constitutes a social order* (Stehr and Ericson 1992). In the broadest and simplest sense, knowledge *refers to any and every set of ideas accepted by a social group or society of people—ideas pertaining to what they accept as real for them* (see, e.g., Berger and Luckmann, 1966, p. 1).

Systems of knowledge are continuously (re)defined by the people who participate in their construction, reproduction, application, and development. I am not suggesting, however, that knowledge in TCs is monochromatic; indeed, as I will demonstrate in chapter 2, pockets of difference exist within systems of knowledge. Individual MA-TESOL programs, for instance, highlight different teaching skills, constrained and influenced as these programs are by local institutional and communal demands and needs. Enrolled TESOLers have their local cognitions shaped by what is available in their immediate environment. All TESOLers—potential L2 teachers, L2 researchers, mentors, scholars—operate within specific parameters of (TESOL) knowledge that are typically made clearer when they are violated than when they are followed. The general argument of this book demonstrates that (L2) teachers-in-training need to know not just what the parameters of their TCs are but what makes up the sometimes divergent pockets of (TESOL) knowledges, constructions, applications, and developments that influence our individual and collective cognitions in both local and not-so-local ways. In this sense, then, the sociology of knowledge seeks to uncover the collective bases from which groups and institutions work toward and compete for positions of authority in the TCs. "Such an inquiry reveals that currents of particular thought [in TCs] are strategic; they originate in group existence and collective action" (McCarthy, 1996), which I discuss in depth in the following sections.

The sociology of TCs concerns itself with two processes: *ways that cultures of TCs are produced* and *ways that cultures of TCs are acquired*. I address elements of both processes, but I am particularly concerned with how, once acquired, the cultures of TCs become the means by which TCs can be viewed and studied to a certain extent as somewhat decontextualized phenomena, relatively distinguishable from the humans who function in them. They are products of our collectives, produced by researchers and scholars, expanded on by institutions, and reinforced by communities of practice. On the other hand, knowledges are also claimed and used by all of us as we go about participating in our TCs (attending classes and conferences, publishing, teaching, researching, writing proposals), where people communicate, perpetuate, and develop their (knowledge about) varied professional skills: teaching, researching, writing theses, mentoring, taking exams—all of the processes involved in fully participating in the collectives. These are processes in which TESOLers, acting with and against each other "in diverse social settings and groups, strive to change or maintain events in the world around them" (McCarthy, 1996), and it is in these processes that ideas regarding awareness and change in TCs are sown and reaped.

Reality construction, diverse as the interpretations of this phrase may be, is linked to what people know and are getting to know, and this knowledge in flux gets communicated, played out, reenacted, and sometimes (marginally) furthered in a multitude of ways. Kaleidoscopic in nature—with shards of knowledge being arranged and rearranged constantly by different TESOL participants in diverse settings—"groups and institutions enter as authorities and arbitrators in the elusive business of defining and grasping part of social reality" (McCarthy, 1996, p. 3). Gaining meta-awareness about what is involved in the knowledge production of TCs is critical for all of us, but it is especially important for teachers and potential teachers because it allows us to see that knowledges determine, in part, the social realities we inhabit by contributing to our sense of social order; to our creating, reproducing, and privileging of some forms over others; and to our making sense of what is "natural" and "commonplace" (in the TCs). As I pointed out in the Introduction, getting TESOLers to recognize that nothing about their profession is value-free is the first step in their realizing that everything about the English-language teaching and learning (ELTL) enterprise is inherently social, cultural, and most definitely political (Benesch, 2001).

TESOL TCs as Activity Systems with Distributed Cognitions and Pockets of Situated Learning

Now I address how TCs connect with theories on activity systems, distributed cognitions, and situated learning. Rather than see one theory as superior to others (in terms of scope, explanatory power, and comprehensiveness), I have amalgamated aspects of them all because each theoretical position affords specific insights into how to conceptualize and understand TCs. What follows is a partial summary of these theories and an explication of some ways they elucidate the notion of TCs. (For comprehensive reviews of these theories, see Lave and Wenger, 1991; Nardi, 1996; Wartenberg, 1990.)

I begin with the foundations of activity theory, whose basic unit of analysis is the "activity." Proponents of this theory generally maintain that constituents of an activity—subject, object, actions—change as conditions and contexts change. The notion of mediation and the tools in the mediating endeavor are primary. The tools are whatever a learner uses in the learning process: artifacts, signs, instruments, language, machines. Situated, historical, and sometimes persistent structures that cut across time and space and that mediate between the human and the world, these tools serve a mediating function between learner and activity and are "created by people to control their own behavior" (Nardi, 1996, p. 75). Thus, it is the relationship connecting the user, artifact, and learning goal that is central to this theory. "People, usually in conjunction with each other and always guided by social norms, set goals, negotiate appropriate means to reach the goals, and assist each other in implementing the means and resetting the goals as activities evolve" (Rogoff and Lave, 1984, p. 4). Context, then, for proponents of this view, is activity itself and vice versa. "People consciously and deliberately generate contexts (activities) in part through their own objects; hence context is not just 'out there'" (Nardi, 1996, p. 76) but is integral to people's relationships with the world.

Exploring the contextualized character of human understanding and communication, theories of distributed cognition and situated learning take as their focal points relationships between learning processes and the social situations in which they are embedded. Lave and Wenger (1991), key proponents of this theory, maintain that learning takes place in a participation framework, not in any individual's mind, and is distributed among coparticipants. A key characteristic of such situated learning is *legitimate peripheral participation*, which, as we saw earlier in the section on discourse communities, refers to the process by which learners get initiated into a community of practitioners as they move toward becoming full participants in the community. Cognitions, then, are located and distributed in the system. The focus is on the coordination of individuals, artifacts, and the communities they are part of—to see these units as part of a whole, with each informing the other's identity—and not on singling out particular units by which to interpret learning. Learning involves the whole person; "it implies becoming a full participant, a member, a kind of person" (Lave and Wenger, 1991, p. 53).

The issue of where cognitions reside—whether in an individual's head or in the context—is of particular importance in this discussion. Luria (1968) and Vygotsky (1962), who can be viewed as early activity theorists, outline ways that tools and symbols mediate between an individual and context, thus shaping and distributing individual and collective cognitions. The term *distribution* connotes a "spreading across" or "stretching over" (Cole and Wertsch, 1996), implying the lack of a single locus or fixed point; it is also a sharing of "authority, language, experiences, tasks, and a cultural heritage" (Saloman, 1993, p. 11)—all features that characterize a TC.

Bateson (1972, p. 459, quoted in Cole and Engestrom, 1997, p. 13) offers the following scenario to capture the intertwined nature of a person's mental makeup, the environment, and the tools used to achieve his or her ends: "Suppose I am a blind man, and I use a stick. I go tap, tap, tap. Where do I start? Is my mental system bounded at the hand of the stick? Is it bounded by my skin? Does it start halfway up the stick? Does it start at the tip of the stick?" Cole, Engestrom, and Vasquez (1997) argue that answers to the questions in this quote change depending on how you think of the event. Cognition, as the quote implies, does not have fixed boundaries or starting and ending points but is distributed across a range of components including the stick and the activities that the blind man is involved in with the stick. Bateson (1972, p. 459, cited in Cole et al., 1997, p. 13) explains: "When the man sits down to eat his lunch, the stick's relation to mind totally changes, and it is forks and knives, not sticks that become relevant. In short, the ways in which mind is distributed depends crucially on the tools through which one interacts with the world, and these in turn depend on one's goals. The combination of goals, tools, and setting . . . constitutes simultaneously the context of behavior and the ways in which cognition gets distributed in that context."

Clearly, then, activity, tools, events, and the complex interactions among them influence local cognitions and mental behavior. In the Bateson quote, the forks and knives serve as tools/mediators that link the person organically and intimately to the world and are more than just filters or channels through which experience gets embodied and consciousness is formed. A person's cognitions are not abstract mental states but states of being that are constantly negotiated, depending partially on the local constraints, available tools (the availability and perhaps preference to eat with forks and knives as opposed to chopsticks or one's fingers), and prevailing social practices of the individual's thought collectives at a given time. Also crucial is the role that sociocultural practices play in shaping mental behavior.

Bateson's reference to forks and knives as if "natural" omits the fact that a person may prefer to eat with his or her fingers, which is an organic and intimate way of relating to the world. What constitutes this preference? Is it the TC that reflects the culture's organization of the reality outside? And why does one culture organize it differently from another, with one group preferring particular eating implements and another preferring different ones or none at all? Although culture can be seen as a uniform, patterned ensemble of beliefs, values, symbols, and tools that people share, it is also very much more heterogeneous than we realize, given how circumscribed it is by local constraints and interactions. Shore (1996), for example, maintains—based on his exploration of how knowledge is distributed across people, generations, occupations, classes, religions, and institutions—that culture is necessarily a distributed phenomenon and has to be understood as such. This tension between patterning and heterogeneity plays itself out in interesting ways in certain kinds of thought collectives—specifically discipline-oriented communities—which can be seen as microcosmic cultural entities that are at once stable and uniform with specific rules, as well as dynamic structures that make room for heterogeneity and difference (Ramanathan and Kaplan, 2000).

Keeping these points in mind, let us turn to how TESOL TCs function as activity systems with distributed cognitions.

According to Fleck (1981), TCs are communities wherein

> thoughts pass from one individual to another, each time a little transformed, for each individual can attach to them somewhat different associations. Strictly speaking, the receiver never understands the thought exactly in the way that the transmitter intended it to be understood. After a series of such encounters, practically nothing is left of the original content. Whose thought is it that continues to circulate? It is one that obviously belongs not to any single individual but to the collective. Whether an individual construes it as truth or error, understands it correctly or not, a set of findings meanders throughout the community, becoming polished, transformed, reinforced, or attenuated while influencing other findings, concept formation, opinions, and habits of thought. (p. 48)

Implied in this quote is the idea that a thought collective is a bidirectional sociocognitive construct that allows us to view participation in it as partially constitutive of participant behavior, responses, and general orientation to the world. Potential teachers have their cognitions and thought processes shaped by a variety of components in the programs, including hallway chats, student-teacher conferences, people, events, and social practices, all of which in turn shape the nature, philosophy, and general direction of the programs. The TESOL discipline can be seen as a larger cocentric circle, reflecting—on a macro scale—social practices similar to those of an average MA-TESOL program. This circle has relative experts, and the potential TESOLer is often partially socialized from the inner circle to the larger one by way of an MA-TESOL degree.

Thought styles, particular viewpoints, ways of approaching issues, and theoretical paradigms are typically communicated from particular pockets in the larger circle to the inner one. Participation in both TCs includes attending classes, fulfilling assignments, doing presentations, publishing in ESL-related journals, presenting at conferences, and participating in TESOL-related administrative tasks. This participation reinforces a bidi-rectional relationship in which the program and discipline par-tially shape the cognitions of L2 student teachers and vice versa. Information regarding relevant tools, activities, and artifacts is transmitted to the novices, and along with interaction with more experienced members of the collectives, novices are inducted into the collectives' practices. Participation in the collectives, in turn, by both experienced members and novices, sustains them.

The description of two TC circles is not intended to suggest a one-way flow of thought styles and viewpoints from experts to novices. Indeed, there exists an intercollective exchange—a com-plex process between (sub)collectives exchanging different view-points that leads to the questioning and sometimes deterioration of fixed systems in the larger circle. As discussed in the section on knowledge in TCs being socially constructed, serious and sus-tained questioning of particular viewpoints creates newer per-spectives—a feature written into the intercollective exchange of thoughts. (Furthermore, there are sub-TCs with their individual thought styles within both circles, although for the purposes of the present study I am limiting my discussion to issues pertinent to the TC of the TESOL discipline and the smaller one of MA-TESOL programs.)

It is in this way that TESOL thought collectives can be seen as activity systems whose cognitions are distributed across a variety of discipline-specific tools and activities that embody a range of features, including particular viewpoints, texts, genres, writing practices, and teaching styles, as well as orientations, jargon terms, and research practices (Ramanathan and Kaplan, 2000), together orienting the participants' thought styles and cognitions in particular directions. The individual participant's knowledge itself is distributed across a range of tangible and intangible dis-ciplinary facets. The fact that I, as researcher, choose to highlight the political and cultural nuances of issues in TESOL is a result of factors distributed over a range of circumstances, past and pres-ent, including the culture in which I grew up, how my own cognitions have been oriented (by particular educational institutions and practices), and the directions in which they are currently evolving, given my present disciplinary associations, my exposure to particular texts (past and present) and pockets of research, and ongoing and developing acquaintances with researchers who reinforce or alter my research stances and ways of interpreting issues in the disciplinary world.

These elements, along with individual program practices, genres, and pedagogical tools, are only some of the various influences that inform how we navigate TCs. Thus, by inviting and sometimes mandating participation in numerous and varied social practices, TCs shape our collective sociocognitive behavior. As we will see in chapter 2, the cultures of local MA-TESOL programs, constrained as they are by departmental, campus-wide, and communal concerns, orient the evolving knowledges/cognitions of enrolled TESOLers in particular ways, distributed as the local cultures are over particular facets, some of which diverge significantly from those in other programs. However, as chapter 3 indicates, we, as participants, influence key aspects of our TCs as well; indeed, as the more general argument of this book goes, it is only when we individually and collectively begin to reflect on and question our key disciplinary practices and our roles in sustaining those practices that we can begin to address issues related to change.

Ideologies in TCs

If TCs operate as activity systems with distinct local and global (sub)cultures, then it follows that they create and sustain particular ideologies. Previous interpretations of *ideologies* have typically used the term to refer to forms of knowing and being in other societies or historical times, which, when seen from our vantage points, appear to be different and perhaps even inimical to our sense of how things should be. McCarthy (1996) points out that common uses of the term *ideology* often get applied to impassioned and doctrinaire group practices. More current uses of the term, however, refer to an assemblage of institutional practices that reinforce and reproduce "the conditions and relations of the industrial capitalist order: its schools, households, trade unions, communications media, its sports and leisure, its courts, its political parties, its universities and so forth" (McCarthy, 1996). Thus, ideologies, in this sense, are evident in a variety of modes—including gestures, attitudes, body language, texts, and particular ways of using language—and everyday actions of groups of people: the foods they eat, the TV shows they watch, the parties they organize, the hairstyles they consider appropriate, or what they use to brush their teeth.

The various ideologies embedded in different knowledges in (TESOL) TCs shape the professional cognitions of all of the organization's participants. In instances when particular knowledges get systematically privileged over others, with support from a range of ancillary sources, the TCs run the risk of this set of knowledges dominating other diverse knowledge pockets. Althusser, who believed that dominant ideologies are linked to the entire social system, also maintained that they function to preserve the status quo, keeping classes and institutions "in the same relative place, performing the same functions, and adapting to the same prevailing conditions" (McCarthy, 1996, p. 39).

When particular facets of TESOL TCs—genres, programs, curricular materials—get systematically aligned in certain ways to promote particular worldviews, it becomes imperative for us as participants to question not just the ideologies themselves but the very facets that hold them in place. It is not just that our TCs create and provide categories by which to organize, distill, and interpret our professional cognitions; in addition, there are groups of "intellectuals"—scholars, researchers, mentors, professors—who employ and give legitimacy to the categories, thus contributing to the acceptance of the TCs' (sub)ideologies as "normal" and neutral. Williams (1976), writing about the relationship between hegemony and the control of cultural resources, points out specific kinds of roles played by educational institutions in sustaining hegemonic ideologies. The following extended quote captures the crux "of how the assemblage of meanings and practices still leads to, and comes from, unequal economic and cultural control" (quoted in Apple, 1990, p. 5):

[Hegemony] is a whole body of practices and expectations. . . . It is a set of meanings and values which as they are experienced as practices appear as reciprocally confirming. It, thus, constitutes a sense of reality. . . . We can understand a . . . culture if we understand the real social process on which it depends: I mean the process of incorporation. The modes of incorporation are of great significance, and incidentally in our kind of society have considerable economic significance. The educational institutions are usually the main agencies of transmission of an effective dominant culture. . . . [A]t a philosophical level . . . there is a process which I call the *selective tradition* . . . the way in which from a whole possible area of past and present, certain meanings and practices are neglected and excluded. Even more crucially, some of these meanings are reinterpreted, diluted, or put into forms which support or at least do not contradict other elements within the effective dominant culture.

The selective tradition that Williams talks about can be seen to exercise a "cognitive authority" (Stehr, 1992) by setting and defending certain normative parameters of what constitutes legitimate knowledge. As we will see in chapters 2, 3, and 4, (sub)ideologies and cultures in the TCs are created, sustained, and reproduced by a range of factors. It is impossible to ever fully disentangle particular knowledges from the social organizations that produce them because content is always affected by the contexts of production. Even though content and context are thus intertwined, we as creators, sustainers, and reproducers of our TCs can and must reflect on, analyze, and question the ways in which our TCs' knowledges are produced and how and what we, as participants, contribute to these endeavors. The following chapters aim to show by example the kind of cross-questioning I mean:

how key facets of our TCs—teacher education programs, particular genres, and pedagogical materials—constitute a set of alignments that we need to rethink, if only to figure out how and where we are moving as a discipline. As Geertz points out:

> The ethnography of thinking, like any other sort of ethnography—of worship, or marriage, or government, or exchange—is an attempt not to exalt diversity but to take it seriously as itself an object of analytic description and interpretive reflection. And as such it poses a threat neither to the integrity of our moral fiber nor to whatever linguists, psychologists, neurologists, primatologists, or artificers of artificial intelligence might contrive to find out about the constancies of perception, affect, learning, or information processing. What it forms a threat to is the prejudice that the pristine powers (to borrow a term from Theodore Schwartz) that we all have in common are more revelatory of *how we think* than the versions and visions (to borrow one from Nelson Goodman) that, in this time or that place, we socially construct. (Geertz, 2000, 154–155, my emphasis)

Chapter 2

The Politics of Local MA-TESOL Programs and Implications for the Larger TC

[T]he unspoken premise from which common sense draws its author-ity—that it presents reality neat—is not intended to undermine that authority but to relocate it. If common sense is as much an interpre-tation of the immediacies of experience, a gloss on them, as are myth, painting, epistemology, or whatever, then it is, like them, his-torically constructed and like them, subjected to historically defined standards of judgment. It can be questioned, disputed, affirmed, developed, formalized, contemplated, even taught, and it can vary dramatically from one people to the next. It is, in short, a cultural system, though not usually a very tightly integrated one, and it rests on the same basis that any other such system rests [on]; the convic-tion by those whose possession it is of its value and validity. Here, as elsewhere, things are what you make of them.

—Clifford Geertz, *Local Knowledge*

Building on the previous chapter's discussion of the sociology of knowledge in TCs and of the complexities underlying notions of common sense, this chapter examines the cultures of two diver-gent MA-TESOL programs in order to show how locally circum-scribed teacher education programs are and how the local cognitions (and by extension common sense) and teaching expertise of enrolled TESOLers are shaped by departmental, cam-pus-wide, and community constraints. Such a comparative analy-sis will allow us to see that smaller TCs, such as individual programs, are activity systems (just as the larger TCs are), with cognitions being distributed across a range of various elements that inform each system. Encouraging enrolled TESOLers to realize that their general evolution as ESL teachers is in many ways shaped by local factors and that their evolving knowledges and expertise diverge—sometimes significantly—from the knowledges and expertise of TESOLers in other programs is the first step in raising their meta-awareness about disciplinary issues.

The question that motivates this chapter, then, is this: What does divergence across various TESOL programs mean for the larger discipline? Based on data gathered by Catherine Davies, Mary Schleppegrell, and myself during 1999 and 2000,[1] this chapter attempts to delineate the extent to which MA-TESOL programs are governed by local exigencies, constraints, and conditions that influence their general direction and slant. Davies, Schleppegrell, and I undertook a study to capture aspects of the cultures of two MA-TESOL programs, located on opposite sides of the United States, to highlight how each program's individual identity is contingent on factors in the local environment and the role that contingency plays in shaping the teaching skills with which enrolled TESOLers graduate. We wanted to address two key issues: (1) how and why particular MA-TESOL programs stress the language teaching skills they do and (2) the implications and consequences of graduating TESOLers from divergent programs on the larger field of TESOL. The general stance toward the programs was not intended to be judgmental; instead, the divergent realities of these two programs were presented with a view to raising consciousness about the implications of these differences for the TESOL discipline by focusing on the institutional context of the MA-TESOL program.

In response to a general push toward standards in education, the TESOL professional organization has recently embarked on an ambitious project to develop standards for teaching in the K–12 context (Snow, 2000; TESOL, 2000). Although these standards certainly have implications for teacher preparation, they focus on defining the skills that ESL students need to develop in primary and secondary schools. The only guidelines for institutions that prepare and certify ESL teachers were developed by the TESOL organization in the late 1960s and early 1970s. These guidelines were intended for programs that certify ESL teachers for U.S. schools, and they are addressed to teacher certification agencies and educational institutions (TESOL, 1997, pp. 284–288). Much has changed, however, in the American social milieu regarding the ESL population since these guidelines were established, and the range of academic and professional competencies that the guidelines propose for a high-quality teacher education program do not address criteria relevant to preparing ESL teachers to teach at tertiary and adult levels, nor are they appropriate for the range of contexts in which ESL/EFL teachers work today (Govardhan, Nayar, and Sheorey, 1999). Also, there have been changes in the kinds of programs offered, from K–12 teacher certification, to certificates on British models, to MA and PhD programs in TESOL.

Further changes have occurred in the opportunities for Americans to teach in EFL contexts and in the degree requirements for better jobs. It would have been impossible for these guidelines to anticipate the range of settings (tertiary levels, refugee contexts, intensive English programs, and workplace settings, to name a few) within which ESL teachers currently work. In particular, these guidelines do not address the range of postsecondary contexts (both within the United States and abroad) for which teachers are currently being prepared in MA-TESOL programs across the country. Concentrating on the context of the MA-TESOL program, this study raises concerns about how idealized and generalizable the current standards are.

Motivations for the Study

The programs under investigation are two that Davies, Schleppegrell, and I know quite well. One is an MA-TESOL program at a California university that we call West Coast University (WCU) and the other a program in the Southeast that we refer to as Southeast University (SEU).[2] The idea for this study came about when I moved from SEU, where I had served as a faculty member and as director of the MA-TESOL program, to the MA-

TESOL program at WCU, where I am currently a faculty member. The transitional process from one program to the other made me realize that although both are MA-TESOL programs, they differ vastly in their curricula, courses, and points of emphasis. Exploring these differences and what they mean for the enrolled potential teachers, then, became an issue worth investigating. Also, Davies and Schleppegrell, the current directors of the two programs, believed, as did I, that doing such a study would embark us all on a critical exercise that would enable us to rethink program goals and design and to suggest possible changes down the road.

Our study was similar to other studies of the cultures/orientations of institutions (e.g., Atkinson and Ramanathan, 1995; Latour, 1986; Ramanathan, 1999; Swales, 1998) in which the focus has been on capturing a holistic sense of how programs/institutions work: what key issues are, how decisions get made and rationalized, what gets emphasized (and what does not), who benefits from particular policies (and who does not), and how outcomes of local negotiations cumulatively impact larger decisions. We also wanted to join a growing body of research that seeks to take a self-reflexive stance on our discipline's practices (C. A. Davies, 1999; C. E. Davies, 1996; Hammersley and Atkinson, 1983; Ramanathan and Atkinson, 1999; Ramanathan and Kaplan, 2000; Schleppegrell, 2001) toward raising meta-awareness (Gee, 1990; Ramanathan, 2001; Wells, 1999) about how we—as full-fledged practitioners in the field—contribute to sustaining program cultures in specific ways to ultimately enable us to effect necessary change.

Aims of the Study

Our primary aim was to gain a global understanding of the ideological underpinnings of both programs. Although the long-term goals of the project include tracing teacher development in key local contexts in the two programs, data collected to date focus on the larger cultures/environments within which enrolled student teachers operate (Agger, 1992; Alasuutari, 1995; Alvesson, 1993; Perryman, 1994). Our focusing on the cultures of the two programs was deliberate: at this stage of the project the primary concern was to lay bare some of the different components that keep the divergent worldviews (Campbell, 1996; Marcus, 1988; Myers, 1988) of the two programs in place, as opposed to analyzing classroom environments and dynamics (a topic that has been addressed extensively; cf. Allwright and Bailey, 1991; Green and Harker, 1983; Woods, 1989). The point of the project was to lay out the larger context—present the two programs, the departments housing them, and institutional/community realities within which the programs and departments operate—before locating and following teachers in the programs. Toward this end we amassed a large database of sources that inform local and not-so-local issues that concern the two programs, including why each program emphasizes what it does and how larger departmental concerns and issues affect decisions and mandates that eventually get reinforced and operationalized. Uncovering some of the complexities involved in how the two programs operate enabled us to better understand the divergent kinds of expertise of our graduating teachers (Freeman, 1996), as well as what such divergences mean for the evolving TESOL discipline.

Issues of Methodology

Although the ethnographically oriented researcher is committed to a sense of the whole, the actual researching process is selective (Atkinson, 1992; Lutz, 1981). The researcher brings, among other things, his or her prior experiences, readings, and theoretical assumptions to the site, all of which necessarily impinge on what the researcher deems noteworthy. The cumulative similarities in our backgrounds and approaches as researchers and teachers influenced how we conceived of the project, what we chose to highlight, and the general direction in which we took the project. At least three features of our individual backgrounds undoubtedly influenced the researching endeavor:

1. We all expected differences between the programs and were thus oriented toward looking for and addressing such differences, since we wanted to focus on the various ways in which ESL teaching and learning evolves in different contexts, with enrolled TESOLers developing teaching skills that reflect the slant of the respective programs. As I mentioned earlier, one of our overall aims was to encourage reflection on how the discipline defines itself and some ways in which different programs contribute to the evolving nature of the profession.

2. As directors of one of the two programs (at different points in our careers), each of us brought an insider's view to the analysis. Individually we had wrestled with issues and decisions that impacted the direction of the programs and sometimes even threatened their very existence. Our roles and positions vis-à-vis the programs and our research endeavor markedly influenced the writing of this manuscript. As Yeatman (1994) points out, "we know reality only via our representations of reality. . . . [Difference of representational perspective] arises out of differences in the positioning of knowing subjects in relation to the historicity of interconnected relationships" (p. 30). All three of us brought different representations of reality to the project.

3. All three of us are committed to a strong, contextualized, situated sense of language and language-related activities, including teaching, learning, and organizational/administrative aspects, and such a perspective shaped how we interpreted the data.

It is against this partial backdrop that the data and their analyses need to be understood.

Data

Collected over the span of a year,[3] the data are of two kinds: (1) the three data types associated with qualitative research, namely, written documents, observations, and interviews, and (2) the less tangible data that each of us had because of our relatively long-term association with at least one of the programs. This latter kind of data was general program-related information we had in our heads about which we conferred with each other and other relevant faculty.

We gathered written documentation from both programs about issues that would help us understand their inner workings. These documents included sample course descriptions, formal and informal descriptions of the two programs, textbooks, teacher training manuals and handouts, graduate student handbooks, admission letters sent out to prospective students, and sample syllabi and assignments. We also interviewed three to four key faculty involved in the programs, including directors of both MA-TESOL and allied programs, the chairs of both departments, and other relevant people.[4] Each interview lasted from 45 to 90 minutes. We made use of field notes I collected during the research process. We asked graduating and advanced students in both programs to answer a questionnaire that covered a range of issues, including what they had gained from the program, the kinds of contexts in which they believed they could teach, and the kinds of teaching skills in which they wished they had more expertise (see appendix A for a complete list of written documentation, who was interviewed and the kinds of questions asked, and a copy of the questionnaire).

As for the less tangible data, we drew on all of the information and experiences that came to us individually and collectively as a result of our familiarity with at least one of the two programs: the history of the programs and issues that had impacted decisions about program design and structure over time, policy issues regarding placement exams, grading, practicum experiences for the developing teachers, information about relations with neighboring/allied departments, admitting students and funding them with available teaching/research assistantship (TA/RA) lines (or not), and the general sequence of courses that students need to take. All of these data types were systematically combed and coded for themes, aspects of which were then interpreted and analyzed. These recurring themes form the crux of the study, and the various subsections in this chapter partially illustrate what these themes are. Both horizontal and vertical dimensions of the data were carefully juxtaposed and analyzed. The horizontal (or historical) dimension "refers to description of events and behaviors as they evolve over time . . . [whereas] the vertical dimension refers to factors which influence behaviors and interactions at the time at which they occur" (Nunan, 1992, p. 58). We attempted to get at historical factors that have shaped the two programs over time and at factors that were being negotiated even as the study was being written up.

Situating the Two Programs

The MA-TESOL Program at West Coast University

The MA-TESOL program at WCU is one of two tracks offered by the Department of Linguistics (general linguistics is the other track). Until the early 1990s, MA-TESOL courses had been split between the Department of Linguistics and the Department of English, the latter handling primarily the teacher training courses. In 1992, TESOL and the university's ESL service courses broke away from English and joined linguistics because the English department "was never very happy with ESL" ("since they [the English department] are interested in literature, not the nuts and bolts of language teaching" [FI 4])[5] and questioned the program's relevance to literary studies (Ramanathan, 1999).

The thrust of the linguistics department before and since MA-TESOL moved in can be said to be largely general and theoretical in nature, with phonology, morphology, syntax, and semantics constituting the core areas that all students in the department have to take. Two assumptions underlay this curricular design: (1) that a strong foundation in linguistics is valuable for language teaching and (2) that these classes will unify all enrolled students, regardless of the track (general or applied) in which they are enrolled (FI 2). Thus, all enrolled MA-TESOL students take a set of general linguistics courses concurrently with the courses required of them in the applied track (see appendix A for a breakdown of required classes). Figure 2.1 provides a visual representation of where the TESOL program is positioned vis-à-vis the linguistics department.

All MA-TESOL students also have to complete a practicum by teaching in the department's ESL program (see fig. 2.1). The ESL

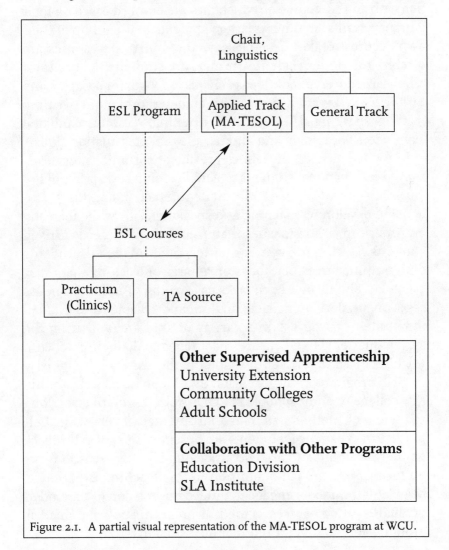

Figure 2.1. A partial visual representation of the MA-TESOL program at WCU.

program serves both graduate (mainly international) and undergraduate (mainly immigrant) students, and enrolled TESOLers are expected to teach "clinics"—that is, small classes comprising about 12 students—concurrently with their first year of TESOL theory and methods courses. These clinics typically meet for an hour twice a week. During the fall quarter, the graduate students who enroll in these clinics are required to take them in conjunction with an ESL course, in which they are enrolled based on their entrance exams. In other quarters students may sign up of their own accord to take these classes, and sometimes clinics are offered for undergraduate immigrant students. The clinics emphasize different points in each quarter, both for students and for the TESOLers. These topics include grammar and writing, reading, speaking skills, academic listening, vocabulary and oral expression, vocabulary and idioms, and oral presentation skills.

In the fall quarter, the clinics provide opportunities for newly arrived international students to gain listening and speaking fluency. They are designed to facilitate interaction and to aid students in developing listening and speaking skills while focusing on American cultural issues that impact them as newly arrived students. During the winter quarter, the MA-TESOL students design minicourses that focus on an area of teaching that interests them and involve such tasks as learning to conduct a needs assessment, developing a curriculum and syllabus, and evaluating students' progress in a variety of skill areas. During the spring quarter, TESOLers are encouraged to do their practicum teaching in a different setting: either in the university's intensive English program (in the extension division) or at a local community college or adult school. TESOLers also enroll in a yearlong sequence of methods courses that interact closely with their practicum experience. Students are observed and given feedback on their teaching and are encouraged to identify areas to focus on for improvement. In addition to this teaching experience, MA-TESOL students engage in guided observation of the undergraduate writing courses in the ESL program and are trained as pronunciation tutors for international students.

In their second year, the enrolled TESOLers may work as TAs, teaching a multiskills ESL course that has a writing component in it. After completing their course work and practicum requirements, MA-TESOL students have the option of either writing a thesis or taking comprehensive exams. About a third of the students choose the thesis option.

The Department of Linguistics comprises eight full-time faculty members, three of whom specialize in applied/sociolinguistics. Ten students were admitted to the department in 1997–1998, and four were admitted in 1998–1999. The program works closely with the education division and a cross-campus Second Language Acquisition Institute, which promotes interaction among students and faculty in the modern languages departments, education, anthropology, and linguistics. Students from these departments also sometimes enroll in the MA-TESOL courses. The MA-TESOL program is one of many ESL teacher education programs in the state and has a different focus from other L2 teacher education programs in the area.

The MA-TESOL Program at Southeast University

The program at SEU is housed in the Department of English, which has historically included several linguists. Unlike the program at West Coast University, linguistics has remained in the same department throughout its existence, although it has been threatened with dissolution at least once in the past. As figure 2.2 indicates, in addition to a traditional literature MA and PhD, the English department maintains an MFA program in creative writing and a certificate and a PhD in rhetoric and composition. The TESOL program is closely allied with the department's rhetoric and composition program, and many of its decisions, including those related to the professional development on teaching assistants, are impacted by what happens in the rhetoric/composition strand. The MA-TESOL program is also closely allied with the university's Intensive Language Institute, a separate unit on campus that provides extensive teaching observation opportunities and a teaching apprenticeship for all MA-TESOL students during their second year in the program. Through some of its course offerings, the MA-TESOL program's institutional links extend to the Department of Modern Languages and Classics' applied linguistics track, to the College of Education's K–12 ESL certification and MA programs, and to its PhD in foreign language education (see fig. 2.2).

Eight semester-long courses in the MA-TESOL curriculum are required courses (see appendix A). The rest of the course work consists of electives: linguistics courses focusing on English (e.g., Structure of English and Dialectology), rhetoric/composition courses, or relevant courses offered in the larger department, as well as courses available through the Department of Modern Languages and Classics, the Department of Anthropology, and the College of Education. The practicum for first-year MA-TESOL students includes attending an intensive weeklong orientation (before the academic year begins) hosted by the rhetoric/compo-

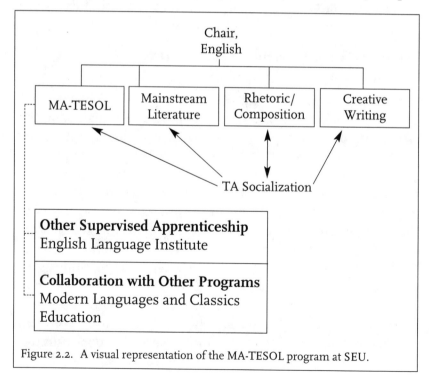

Figure 2.2. A visual representation of the MA-TESOL program at SEU.

sition strand (see fig. 2.2) on teaching composition, after which they are typically assigned as coteachers to nonnative sections of composition.[6] TAs are apprenticed as coteachers under a main teacher (a TA who has taught composition for at least a year) for their first year, after which they become main teachers, socializing other coteachers into teaching (L1 and/or L2) composition.[7]

All composition classes—native speaking and ESL—at SEU are offered as a sequenced unit, with the first course (101/120) focusing on various aspects of academic writing (including effective use of voice, moves, and various modes of writing) and the second (102/121) concentrating on the teaching and learning of writing based on English literature (where students are exposed to a variety of literary genres and ways of writing about them). These sections are observed by faculty, and TAs are given feedback on their teaching. TAs are required to attend weekly sessions throughout the year on pedagogical issues that arise in their classrooms. Simultaneously, they are required to enroll in two writing-related graduate courses to give them a theoretical background and practical guidance focusing on ESL writing and reading. The students who make up the ESL sections of composition are largely international students placed into these sections after clearing a placement exam that tests their oral and written proficiency.

To counterbalance the practicum's focus on the teaching of writing, in their second year MA-TESOL students at SEU are also required to observe a range of classes at the university's English Language Institute (ELI) and typically do supervised teaching of spoken language skills. They express preference for a course and level and are matched with a mentor teacher. During the first eight weeks of the semester, they observe the course that they will be teaching during the second eight weeks. In addition, they observe a range of other courses and levels and participate in supplementary activities and ELI faculty meetings. During the second eight weeks, they assume responsibility for their course and receive feedback from their mentor teacher and from MA-TESOL faculty. All MA-TESOL students must take comprehensive exams, typically during their fourth semester in the program, but they have the option of either writing a thesis or taking two additional courses. Most students choose the latter.

Typically, five to seven students have been admitted to the program each year. Forty-one new students were admitted to the department in 1998–1999, seven of whom were MA-TESOL students. There are 33 full-time faculty members in the English department, of whom three are associated with the MA-TESOL program. Unlike the program at WCU, the program at SEU is the only one of its kind in the state (excluding certificate or certification programs) because of a system-wide ban on program duplication. The program, however, accommodates some students from a K–12 program run out of the College of Education as well as those from Modern Languages and Classics on the same campus.

Differences between the Programs

Although the two programs differ in their local concerns, some key issues cut across both programs. Each program has addressed these issues differently because of local circumstances and local constraints. The following sections deal with how the two MA-TESOL programs negotiate their general status within and across departments; ways in which the programs' course offerings, practicum experiences, and disciplinary frameworks differ from each other; and issues common to both programs, regardless of local constraints.

Negotiating the Status of MA-TESOL within and across Departments

A dominant theme that emerges from faculty interviews in both programs has to do with ways that each program has had to negotiate its status within the department in which it is (and has been) housed, as well as its relation to similar programs in the university. Both programs have had to contend with this issue but in very different ways. The English department at SEU created the MA-TESOL program in the mid-1980s. The status and general validity of the TESOL program was debated a few years ago when the entire English department faculty had to vote on whether to continue the program. The issue was truly local and was linked partly to personnel issues: retaining faculty who "fit" in an English department and who could maintain productive relations with collaborative units on campus.

Some members of the faculty believed that the pedagogical orientation of the program and its perceived social science bias made it an uncomfortable fit for the English department and that it rightfully belonged elsewhere. This view gradually changed, however, as the rhetoric and composition people in the department had to develop pedagogically oriented courses to accompany the teaching of Composition 101 and 102—an emphasis that has comported well with the MA-TESOL program's relatively pedagogical focus. The program sometimes has to negotiate its status by competing for TA-ships with the other strands in the department, depending on the number of students it admits each year.[8] The program is careful to admit only students with TA-ships to ensure that all students receive the practicum experience integral to its focus.

The program has also had to negotiate its status with other departments and colleges in the university. The dozen or so linguists at SEU are located in four colleges and seven departments; there is no formal linguistics department or program. As both Modern Languages and Classics (in the College of Arts and Sciences) and Curriculum and Instruction (in the College of Education) have responded to student interest and state needs and requirements respectively, they are negotiating with the MA-TESOL program to use its courses as part of their requirements (while also creating courses that the MA-TESOL students can take).

The program at WCU has also had to negotiate its general position. The issue of where it belonged came up in 1992, when the English department, of which it was a part, voted for it to move to the linguistics department, which saw it as a natural fit given that the MA students were already earning the degree in the linguistics department.[9] Interviews with the chair of the linguistics department and with ESL instructors (who were then in English but are now in the linguistics department) reveal that ESL (and the teacher education courses that were part of English) had little standing in the English department. "We were a very small part of the composition program and as we got more and more students we had to ask for a budget from the head of composition, who didn't necessarily know anything about the rationale of what we were doing" (FI 4). The general area of ESL instruction and ESL issues was at the "bottom of the heap," and "we were relegated off to this corner"[10] (FI 4) because "we were all linguists by training and they were all English literature people and there was a real difference in the understanding of what we were doing" (FI 4).

Consequently, ESL was in a constant fight for existence. Since its move to the linguistics department, however, the MA-TESOL program has not really had to deal with a legitimacy issue. If it has come up at all, it has been in relation to the general linguistics component that all students in the TESOL track have to take. There have been instances when the program has had to justify its required general linguistics courses, most especially to some TESOLers, who have expressed reservations that courses in syntax, phonology, and morphology have any value in their ultimate pursuit of becoming teachers. In recent years, however, several of the general linguistics faculty "have edged their courses in directions that are more relevant to the applied students" (F2 4). Regarding pressure to establish its legitimacy in relation to other departments, the program at WCU has not faced any threat of duplication thus far. Education students who need course work for ESL certification get it through a course in the MA-TESOL program.

MA-TESOL programs are typically housed in other larger departments. Both programs under examination here have had to negotiate their status and overall purpose in relation to prevailing currents and tensions in their respective departments. Their identities partially hinge on contacts with and changes resulting from issues that concern the larger department of which they are a part, a point that becomes clearer in the following section on local departmental constraints.

Divergent Courses, Practicums, and Disciplinary Frameworks

That both programs have distinct takes on L2 teacher education is evident in a variety of ways, including (1) the ways each program justifies its course offerings and practical training for its enrolled TESOLers and (2) the discipline-specific explanatory frameworks that inform the general functioning of each program (Atkinson and Ramanathan, 1995). The data reveal that the programs' differences are sustained because of several local and disciplinary contingencies operating within each MA-TESOL program, some of which are departmental and/or campus-wide in nature. Separating departmental concerns from disciplinary ones is in some cases impossible because each is intertwined and embedded in the other. These concerns are thus to be interpreted as wholes. Instances where we have teased some of these strands apart should be read as an effort to isolate and understand some of the various factors feeding into the complex picture.

Justification for course offerings and practical training for MA-TESOL at WCU. As I mentioned earlier, the program at WCU mandates a required number of courses in general linguistics, along with required applied linguistics courses. The general understanding for such a course layout is that students need to know their linguistics basics and that such an understanding will aid their ultimate professional development. As the director of the program maintains: "The focus on language is really useful for them as ESL teachers, both here and overseas. I think it gives them a foundation that's different from a program that's a lot more pedagogically oriented with courses on teaching reading or speaking skills. . . . I think the students that come here want that focus on language, the structure of language and understanding language more deeply and that's what they get here" (FI 1). This justification works well given the way the program at WCU has integrated itself into the linguistics department and the way core classes are seen as the unifying thread holding the applied and general tracks together.

The general linguistics orientation to the MA-TESOL program partially stems from its local accommodation to and with the interests of the larger department. Issues related to the practicum of the MA-TESOL students feed into the worldview of this program as well and seem to be just as constrained by local factors. What gets taught in the clinics, for instance, and why, is contingent on factors such as the structure of the course that the clinic students are taking during the fall quarter and the hourly sessions, twice a week, that limit the teachers' ability to address particular facets of language skills. For example, because clinic students see these as less formal than their other university courses, the teachers are unable to ask them to do homework assignments. This means that teaching, for example, the rhetorical aspects of academic writing (which requires intensive homework and more time both in and outside of class) is almost impossible to do (FI 1). Thus, most clinics are designed around skills that can be addressed given these local time constraints: building academic vocabulary for academic writing, working on writing issues at the paragraph level, and addressing issues related to teaching speaking and listening skills (developing pronunciation skills or building spoken vocabulary). Another local factor that influences the writing taught in the clinics is the fact that WCU is, to a large extent, a sciences institution. Students taking the clinics are by and large science students who expect to use writing in certain discipline-specific ways.

The practical experience that the MA-TESOL students receive from teaching clinics justifies for the university its continued support of the general ESL program, on the basis that clinics serve as a training ground and research site for graduate students in TESOL (a factor that contributes to the legitimacy of the ESL program as well). The questionnaires filled out by three (out of four) of the graduating/advanced students mention that they view these teaching skills as valuable, especially for the overseas contexts, community colleges, and intensive language programs in which they expect to work after graduation.

Discipline-specific explanatory frameworks at WCU. The larger disciplines that seem to inform most issues in the program at WCU, including course content, curricular design, and practicums, appear to be education, sociolinguistics, and general linguistics. The overall tilt of the program toward these disciplines results from several dynamic and evolving factors that operate in the program: individual faculty interests, close ties with the education department on campus, the existence of a second language acquisition focus on campus more broadly, and the larger issues that emerge from the political landscape in the state where the university is located.

Within the program disciplinary orientations get worked out in specific contexts, including how course content highlights certain themes more than others. The presence of education credential students in TESOL classes, for example, has pushed instructors to orient the classes in ways that address this population's (largely K–12) needs. On the other hand, the presence of students from the language departments, especially Spanish, has oriented the second-language-acquisition courses and new seminars that have been developed toward issues of bilingualism, classroom research, and first-language writing for academic contexts. Involvement of the faculty in graduate committees in the education department and the language departments is yet another reason for these disciplines to play a key role in the culture of the TESOL program ("I was asked to join the education graduate group and thus started working more with students in education" [FI 1]). Collaboration between faculty in linguistics and the language departments has promoted the second-language-acquisition focus on activities such as organizing conferences, bringing in speakers, and coordinating course offerings to make the best use of faculty with interests in this area across departments.

In addition, the content of TESOL courses at WCU is partially dictated by education-related issues dominant in the state: teacher sensitivity to immigrant issues, bilingualism, and heightened awareness about ESL issues at the K–12 levels. Issues related to English as a foreign language have also been a major focus of the program because many students come from EFL contexts and plan to teach in such contexts upon graduation. Because of pressing local issues, however, this program, which once leaned toward EFL issues ("developing programs for specific-purposes kinds of contexts" [FI 1]), finds itself increasingly concerned with serving the local needs and contexts of the immigrant population. Pressure from enrolled and former students also has an impact on the program's focus as students report on the questions they are asked at job interviews and provide information about the contexts in which they get jobs after graduating. They continue to ask for more instruction in teaching grammar, for example, even after focus on pedagogical grammar was incorporated into the methods courses in response to their demands. Other issues that remain in focus as a result of students' feedback include ways to encourage learner-centered classrooms and a greater emphasis on the teaching of writing skills. The evolving issues that inform curricular decisions, then, are largely determined by the kinds of interaction that occur among campus faculty and the perceived needs of the enrolled students and the community at large, which in turn inform the culture of the program.

Justification for course offerings and practical training for MA-TESOL at SEU. Issues related to course offerings and practical training work quite differently at SEU, although like WCU, decisions regarding them are heavily influenced by the local needs and concerns of the larger department, especially those related to rhetoric and composition. As I mentioned previously, the MA-TESOL program at SEU has close ties with this strand in the department and runs the ESL sections of composition under its general auspices. Although the MA-TESOL program is in charge of the ESL sections of composition—for instance, it chooses what it regards as appropriate textbooks for ESL composition and has its own pedagogically oriented courses—the TESOLers are socialized with all other TAs in the department during summer orientation. All TESOLers in their first year are also expected to take an additional one-hour course (per week) that addresses the peda-gogical aspects of teaching a "native" section.

As with WCU, curricular decisions and practicum require-ments have been, to a large part, worked out to accommodate and serve both larger departmental and local MA-TESOL needs: the department needs to have several ESL sections of composition because all undergraduate international students—like their native English-speaking classmates—must take two semesters of composition; the enrolled TESOLers meet part of their practicum requirements by teaching these sections of composition. Thus, the identity of the MA-TESOL program in the department is par-tially justified in terms of this service, which is implicit in the composition director's comments about the role of TESOL: "International students have different needs. They really do need specially trained people with backgrounds in TESOL. . . . The last thing I wanted to do was put graduate students not particularly trained to teaching native speakers into a class where they would regard the errors of nonnative speakers with the same sort of jaundiced view that they regard those from their native-speaking students" (FI 23). Thus, the practical expertise that the TESOLers acquire is partially tied to what the department needs to accom-plish vis-à-vis the larger campus needs—a link that helps hold the program in place.

The practical emphasis on teaching (L2) writing is mirrored by the theoretical thrust of two required courses that have to do with issues related to teaching ESL composition (see course require-ments in appendix A). These are courses that TESOL TAs take dur-ing their first two semesters to receive both practical and theoretical instruction about the ESL sections of composition that they are currently teaching. Given this general layout, teaching-related problems that arise among the TAs are largely writing ori-ented, with issues of plagiarism, writing workshops, and the drafting process being some areas where the TAs need help and supervision. To counteract the general leaning of the program toward writing-related issues, the director of the TESOL program frequently advises students to "gain as much teaching experience as possible in other contexts" (FI 21), including tutoring ESL children in the city schools and observing and teaching a non-writing-related class at the English Language Institute during their apprenticeship there. Indeed, most of the TESOLers opt to teach a speaking class during their semester at the language institute.

Discipline-specific explanatory frameworks at SEU. The larger disciplines informing issues in the program at SEU seem to be rhetoric and composition and sociolinguistics. Their influence can be seen in courses offered, curricular design, and choice of textbooks. The slant on writing that pervades the program and department in general reflects the philosophy of writing that the director of composition upholds, which gets translated into key sites of TA socialization (in summer orientation or the yearlong pedagogical course that 101/102 TAs have to take). One central issue that the director emphasizes is the notion of voice in writing and its general importance in a liberal education: "I like students to be able to develop not just one voice but a number of voices in their writing and this is not an academic voice, a kind of voicelessness, a generic voice. . . . I want them to know that the subject of their composition is their take on the subject of their composition. It is an original thing that has to happen, and if it doesn't happen, it's not worth writing and it's not worth reading" (FI 23).

Writing/composition is seen as an exercise whereby students (TAs and the students they teach) learn to resist "being dominated by the texts." The emphasis on literature in Composition 102 exists because "literature brings something to a liberal arts education that is essential in distinguishing it from other departments. It's part of what people need to learn to call themselves educated" (FI 23). This approach to writing informs the general culture of the MA-TESOL program and, to some extent, the way ESL writing is conceptualized and taught. Accompanied by a strong sociolinguistic slant from the TESOL faculty, such an approach to writing—where all writing-related issues in courses are located and discussed against a social backdrop—fits well with the socially conscious ideology of the English department. The linguistics courses and TESOL special topics courses also tend to be discourse oriented and serve to balance the writing focus.

As at WCU, students coming in from other programs have had some effect in shaping courses, for example, taking more account of content-based ESL instruction for K–12 contexts in a basic TESOL methods course and adapting a second-language development course to include data from languages other than English. Faculty have become involved in graduate committees for students in other departments and colleges, facilitating more networking and leading to informal meetings about curricula and programs in order to make the best use of resources across the university. The southeastern context, with its influx of Spanish and German speakers, as well as the development of other language communities, is influencing the program. Feedback from graduates, especially from EFL contexts, has helped. For example, input from one graduate hired to teach at a German university was a major impetus in the creation of a pedagogical grammar course.

Common Issues

Despite these divergent worldviews, given each program's individual negotiations with local departmental and communal concerns, a small set of ongoing interests relevant to both programs emerged from our data. These have to do with (1) common local factors in both programs that sustain individual program cultures and (2) common ongoing questions/conflicts in both programs.

Common Local Factors Influencing Both Program Cultures

Faculty interests in research and teaching. Faculty in both programs recognize that their own evolving individual research and teaching interests cumulatively (and partially) shape and sustain the culture of the programs and influence everything from course offerings (depending on the background and research expertise of faculty) to course design (where the research focus of faculty informs their general take on the field) to key issues in the field that get highlighted (where faculty members choose to highlight specific research domains over others). The director of the program at WCU initially oriented the program toward EFL issues because that was one of her research strengths until more recently, when she found herself getting interested in issues related to bilingualism and the immigrant student population. This evolving interest, combined with an increase in the number of education students taking TESOL courses, led to an increased emphasis on issues related to immigrant education. The hiring of a new faculty member with strengths in rhetoric and composition is leading to the development of new courses in literacy and the teaching of writing. Likewise, at SEU the director's orientation toward spoken language, sociolinguistics, and cross-cultural issues has influenced the (L2) writing context of that program.

On the other hand, faculty sometimes try to maintain the existing culture of a program which is especially evident in the hiring process. When WCU recently hired a new person, the department wanted to hire someone who would share and strengthen the pedagogical aspects of the program so that the practicum experience, considered central to the development of the TESOLers by both students and faculty, would be supported and strengthened. SEU, in a recent job search, was clear that it wanted a TESOL person with research and teaching interests in L1/L2 composition because such a person fit into the culture of the existing program given its orientation toward writing. The general sentiment seemed to be that such a candidate would also work well with the rhetoric/composition strand in the department, with which the MA-TESOL program is closely allied. Clearly, then, faculty interests shape program cultures in different ways, sometimes by extending the prevailing culture in new directions, at other times ensuring that the current culture is not (too) threatened by new and radically different faculty interests.

Initiating new faculty by sharing sample syllabi and course readings is yet another instance of faculty members working to keep the existing culture in place. If we view written documents such as syllabi as artifacts that are in place because they respond to certain departmental/community needs (Ramanathan and Kaplan, 2000), then we can see that sharing them becomes a way to initiate new faculty into local concerns and needs. It also becomes a way to keep important traces of the existing culture in place.

Jobs graduating TESOLers seek and get. The kinds of jobs that graduating TESOLers seek and get also influence the general slant of the two programs. The students graduating from SEU's program typically pitch themselves as having expertise in teaching writing and generally apply for jobs overseas or in language institutes where such skills are prioritized. Likewise, students graduating from the program at WCU apply for jobs in language teaching contexts for which they feel they have gained relevant experience: intensive language programs, EFL contexts, and community colleges. The notes/letters received from many of these graduated students describing their job experiences shape, to some extent, curricular decisions in the programs, either to strengthen an area that already works or to revise an area that needs improvement (pedagogical grammar, for instance, seems to be one focus that both programs recently instituted because of frequent requests from students). The directors of both programs have also received communications from graduates working in a variety of contexts—intensive English institutes, composition programs, community colleges, refugee programs—that serve to reinforce prevailing program cultures.

Common Questions in Both Programs

Our data revealed that both programs were wrestling with similar long-term questions: How might an MA-TESOL program most effectively balance pedagogic and research-oriented interests? What kinds of contexts should the program be preparing graduates for? This section attempts to address some ongoing questions with which both programs find themselves contending.

The tension between teaching and research. Both SEU and WCU are committed to the idea that MA-TESOL programs are teacher education programs whose ultimate aim is to prepare teachers to teach English effectively. Both programs also wrestle with the issue of the extent to which potential teachers need to be exposed to research and the researching process. The director of the program at SEU maintains that "this conflict reflects, in part, a split in the field of TESOL" (FI 21). Both programs see themselves as responsible for encouraging critical and theoretical reflection on the pedagogic practices engaging their TESOLers (Ramanathan, 2001; Richards and Lockhart, 1996; Schleppegrell, 1997); both programs discourage applicants who appear to conceptualize TESOL as learning a "bag of tricks" (FI 21). This critical reflection partially emerges from an ongoing interaction among the various theoretical perspectives encountered by students in their courses and their teaching experiences.

Both programs are obligated to provide a set of principles about language and learning that can be adapted to any context because their graduates have found themselves teaching in extremely varied circumstances. But at what stage are the programs emphasizing theory over practice or vice versa? And to what extent is the emphasis a result of local conditions and constraints? The program at SEU, given its history, is careful not to appear too pedagogically oriented so that it will not lose prestige within the department; it is also concerned with how to collaborate most productively with the university's College of Education, which is not focused primarily on ESL. Likewise, the program at WCU has had to emphasize its research orientation to justify funding for the ESL program with which it interacts and to encourage students to engage in independent research projects; on the other hand, it emphasizes its pedagogical orientation to counterbalance the heavy structural linguistics component.

One issue that could affect the balance of research and pedagogy is the emerging PhD concentrations that will be affiliated with both programs. The general process of thinking through the various components of a PhD proposal—a project with which both faculties have been concerned in recent years—has the relevant faculty wondering about whether the presence of a research-oriented program, such as the PhD, will affect the two MA-TESOL programs. As the director of the program at SEU puts it, the presence of the PhD "provides an opportunity for the MA-TESOL people to become more involved with research, so research may receive more emphasis in relation to practice" (FI 21).[11] The program at SEU, whose PhD program is already underway, is likely to test the validity of this claim sooner than WCU, which is still in the planning stages of its PhD proposal. It is possible that the presence of a PhD program may alter the existing balance between teaching and research in the two programs.

The challenge of preparing students for a range of contexts. As I mentioned previously, the design of each program's curriculum is partially dictated by issues related to the job market, as well as by the changing needs of local communities. The nature of the jobs that graduating TESOLers seek and have gotten in the past influence the programs' orientations toward preparing students for teaching in different situations and in different skill areas and for focusing on ESL or EFL teaching contexts. Knowledge about the kinds of jobs available (within the United States or overseas), the type of institutions seeking teachers (English-language institutes, community colleges, writing programs, K–12 school districts), and the demand for particular language skills (speaking vs. writing, for instance) contribute to shaping the programs.

Local community needs affect both programs. The program at SEU, for example, has seen the international population of the local area and the state increase dramatically. There is heightened awareness of the need for ESL-sensitive teachers at K–12 and tertiary levels within the community (with ESL teacher certification being instituted in the College of Education only recently to meet this need). The SEU program, however, also has a significant number of international and American graduates teaching in EFL contexts, which keeps pressure on the program to maintain a focus on overseas teaching as well. The program at WCU, in contrast, has always operated within a multicultural local and state context, with sister institutions preparing teachers with training in ESL. Its graduates find jobs in ESL and EFL settings. In particular, WCU needs to accommodate "a lot of nonnative speakers [enrolled in the program] who are going to be teaching in EFL contexts" (FI 1)—international students who will return to their home countries after earning an MA-TESOL degree to enhance their job status. The students in both programs who responded to the questionnaire said that they believed the program gave them the background they needed for both ESL and EFL teaching. Clearly, however, both programs face a significant challenge in providing appropriate preparation for the wide range of contexts in which their graduates will teach.

Discussion, Implications, and Conclusions

Although this project began with a small set of questions—primarily centering on the idea of divergent MA-TESOL cultures and the implications of such divergence on the larger field of TESOL—the researching process brought to light an array of related albeit unanticipated issues. Most of these issues have been addressed in the preceding pages, but I would like at this point to summarize and recast our key findings against a larger backdrop.

Assuming the color of a larger department. One key issue that emerges and echoes all through the data-gathering and reflecting process is the realization of how deeply integrated MA-TESOL programs are in the larger departments of which they are a part. Unlike other disciplinary entities such as anthropology or physics, MA-TESOL programs in general have had to gain much of their status and identity from the larger departments that house them. This may be in part because TESOL, as a discipline, has not been around nearly as long as disciplines devoted to physics or anthropology and is thus a fledgling discipline in many ways. Both of the programs examined here are clearly influenced by their host departments, which reveals itself in a variety of ways, including the emphasis on writing/composition at SEU and the structural component of the required courses at WCU. Both programs are also under implicit pressure to conform to the prevailing ideologies of the larger departments: the program at SEU cannot afford to be too pedagogical lest it be seen as belonging elsewhere; the curriculum at WCU has to be structurally oriented because it belongs in a general linguistics department. Although we do not question the overall hue of individual TESOL programs—there is, after all, nothing inherently right or wrong about TESOL programs belonging to English or linguistics (or any other department)—the fact that they do get thus "varnished" is worth noting because it underscores the idea that (MA-)TESOL is not as much a self-defined identity as we may think it is. On the contrary, it appears chameleon-like, with individual program cultures evidencing marked traces of their larger departments.

Despite this general tendency to be influenced by larger departments, the two programs possess a degree of inherent dynamism and flexibility. Their cultures are constantly being tweaked and extended in different directions. As our data revealed, departmental constraints and pressures and larger community needs, along with the kinds of students taking TESOL classes, influence course content and the general program direction. Thus, the cultures of individual MA-TESOL programs have little choice but to adjust, accommodate, and evolve in response to the immediate needs in front of them.

Divergent expertise with which L2 teachers graduate. The teaching skills with which potential teachers graduate from the two programs and the kinds of contexts they are ready for when they leave seem clearly tied to local constraints as well: the clinics at WCU are structured to prioritize the development of certain teaching skills (given the time constraints) over others just as the intense socialization that TAs at SEU receive regarding their teaching composition highlights this one language skill over others. Other local factors—such as individual and cumulative faculty interests, the highlighting of some L2 domains over others, and a general tilt toward ESL or EFL—play into the background of enrolled TESOLers as well. Both programs are thus producing ESL teachers with fairly different backgrounds and teaching abilities.

Implications for the Larger Field of TESOL

These local differences and common concerns bring us to the larger question with which this study began: What implications do such differences have on the general field of TESOL? Clearly the two programs are graduating teachers with different areas of teaching expertise. If both programs are partially representative of programs across the United States, then the issue emerges of whether TESOL needs to establish some criteria for what graduating TESOLers should be able to do at the tertiary and adult levels. The current "Guidelines for Certification and Preparation" for TESOL teachers (last revised in 1975!) lists a set of "objectives and features of a teacher-education program in teaching English as a Second Language," but nowhere does it specify the kind of teachers the list targets. Is it aimed at K–12 teachers? Or tertiary-level teachers? Adult immigrant contexts? Under the section titled "Pedagogy" it specifies that ESL teacher education programs should offer "[f]oundations, methods, practicum—courses and training with the primary objective of providing theoretical and methodological foundations, and practical experience leading to competence in actual teaching situations" (reprinted in TESOL, 1997).

Both programs meet these requirements. They provide sound theoretical underpinnings and foundations for practicum courses, and they introduce students to actual teaching situations. As we have seen, however, both programs achieve this goal in markedly different ways. It could be argued that TESOL as a discipline has deliberately tried to remain open-ended and thus somewhat unspecific about its objectives so as to accommodate divergent programs such as the ones examined in this chapter because it recognizes that MA-TESOL programs exist in a variety of different departments with different local needs. However, several questions remain: Is the divergent expertise of our graduating teachers what the certification guidelines committee had in mind when it came up with the criteria in 1975? What implications does such divergence have on the larger field of TESOL? Given all of the various constraints—local, departmental, campus-wide, budgetary concerns, individual faculty interests—what are our ultimate goals for our students? Is it possible to formulate those goals in such a way that MA-TESOL programs will ensure that all graduates have a common set of skills? Should standards be developed that can be adopted by programs in a variety of contexts? Or do prospective employers of MA-TESOL graduates need to investigate the kinds of skills offered by a particular program, to see whether those graduates have been adequately prepared to meet the challenges the employer faces?[12]

These questions raise the larger issue crucial to all of us in TESOL—but particularly to enrolled TESOLers—namely, whether MA-TESOL is a unitary field for which general standards can be developed or whether it should be thought of as a profession toward which each program that prepares teachers will take a different slant and specialization. It is important that teachers-in-training are encouraged to cultivate critical and analytic reflection on the practices of their discipline. As the quote heading this chapter reminds us, "the unspoken premise from which common sense draws its authority . . . is historically constructed . . . and can be questioned, disputed, affirmed, developed, formalized, contemplated, even taught." It is crucial for all language teachers to engage in peeling away the layers that make up the common sense or the natural if only to understand how their knowledges/cognitions are being shaped. Encouraging this meta-awareness of their socialization process is the first step toward making them critical, proactive educators.

Chapter 3

The Politics of Genres and Text Types

Genre knowledge is . . . best conceptualized as a form of situated cognition embedded in disciplinary activities.
—Berkenkotter and Huckin, *"Rethinking Genre"*

Although not all knowledges in our TCs are created, distilled, and disseminated through particular written forms or even, for that matter, through writing, vast portions of them are. Locating the discussion in the realm of L2 writing, I address the importance of making TESOLers meta-aware of the genres and text types through which they mediate access to knowledge pockets in their TCs.

The debate regarding the role of genre instruction in L2 writing has typically put advocates for and against form-focused instruction in what seem like mutually exclusive camps. In one camp are researchers (Berkenkotter and Huckin, 1993; Christie, 1993; Cope and Kalantzis, 1993; Johns, 1995) who maintain that genre instruction becomes a way by which *all* students—including those from historically marginalized groups—are exposed to "the ways in which the 'hows' of text structure produce the whys of social effect," thus allowing them equal access to a "variety of realms of social power" (Cope and Kalantzis, 1993, p. 8). In the other camp are scholars who accord more importance to the writer and the actual process of writing (Raimes, 1991; Zamel, 1984) than to elements of genre and organization because they believe these elements get addressed anyway in the process of (re)writing. In this chapter I discuss the importance of sensitiz-

ing potential L2 teachers—especially those who may find themselves teaching writing at tertiary levels—to genre-related issues.
Specifically, I discuss the need to orient L2 student teachers to
ways that text structures—the ones they are in the process of
acquiring and those that they are teaching—either remain stable
or evolve over time. Such awareness will heighten their general
meta-awareness of their profession.

I begin by discussing some general connections between the
social notions of genre and author before addressing the complex
relation between genre and discourse community. None of these
terms—*genre, author, discourse community*—can be fully understood apart from the others, and although a comprehensive examination of each term is not provided (for in-depth discussions, see
Cope and Kalantzis, 1993; Ferris and Hedgcock, 1998; Kirsch and
Roen, 1990; Penrose and Geisler, 1994; Rafoth, 1990), links
between them are suggested. Although some of the discussion on

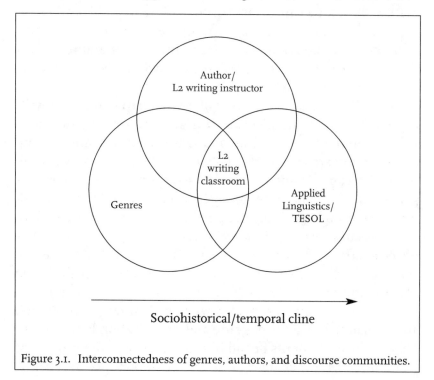

Figure 3.1. Interconnectedness of genres, authors, and discourse communities.

TCs in this chapter is drawn from research on discourse communities, the two expressions are not used interchangeably. As I pointed out in my Introduction, definitions of *discourse community* have typically revolved around texts, places, and groups, whereas the focus of TCs is on the (evolving) professional/disciplinary cognitions of their participants. Next, I address ways that social practices within disciplines—particularly the applied linguistics/TESOL field—work to stabilize particular textual forms. I then explore the generally dynamic nature of genres and address ways that genres evolve within disciplines and across time. In the final section, I discuss the importance of encouraging meta-awareness partially through genre sensitivity among (L1 and) L2 writing instructors. (See fig. 3.1 for a visual representation of the interconnectedness of these terms.)

Genres and Authors

Any social theory of language has to account for how particular conventions give rise to texts of a more or less predictable nature. The routinized greeting of two people meeting and talking casually ("Hi, how're you?" "I'm fine, thanks. And you?") is a case in point. As recognizable and often repeated as the basic structure of this exchange is, it becomes a way by which social relationships get codified and to some extent sustained. The conventional aspect of this interaction is what we recognize as generic—as making of this text a particular genre (Kress and Hodge, 1979). Theories on spoken and written genres make explicit the social conventions and insider knowledge that contribute to the particular forms of certain texts. These theories attempt to show, in part, what kinds of social contexts produce such texts and the overall meanings of these texts.

Before we can comprehend the social nature of texts fully, we must recognize the social nature of the author (Horner, 1997). Williams (1977) identifies three levels on which the author can be recognized as a social being. The first involves a recognition that authors operate in a "political economy of writing" (p. 36), that they write to earn a living drawn partly from "available institutions of patronage, the print market, and the modes of distributing their work" (p. 36); the second level is the recognition that authors "employ socially inherited forms—a language and written conventions and notations—to achieve ends still understood to be self-determined" (p. 37); and the third level (one that is seldom addressed) is the recognition that "the contents of [an author's] consciousness are socially produced" (p. 37). At the first two levels the author is still a somewhat distinct, autonomous individual; issues regarding the economy of publication are "imagined to be mere historical 'background'" (p. 37)—factors exterior to the writer. It is only at the third level that the author's individual autonomy is truly questioned.

There has been a tendency—especially in composition studies—to uphold the autonomous author, to downplay his or her "social consciousness" (Horner, 1997). Such an understanding of authors, however, elides the fact that individuals are to a large extent a result of their engagement in social practices; that they embody a meeting point of several, sometimes competing, social forces and discourses (Gee, 1990). Thus, it is not just that the author deals with the social world; it is, as Horner maintains, that *the author's consciousness itself is socially produced. Thus, any writing or negotiating of writing in any context in which the author engages is invariably primarily social.* As we will see, such a holistic, social view helps explain the deeply dialogic (Bakhtin, 1986; Prior, 1995) relations between genres and the TCs that sustain them.

Genres, TCs, and Stability

If, as I have proposed, everything about the author's consciousness is socially formed, then it follows that the genres in which authors engage do not just emerge from their heads but are socially formed as well. Kamberelis (1995, p. 119) points out that "systems of genres develop within social formations that represent the ways in which those social formations have constructed an infinite number of discourse possibilities into a relatively small set of conventionalized codifications." Within the applied linguistics/TESOL disciplines such conventionalized codifications include writing (and reviewing) abstracts; making conference presentations; and writing articles, books, and grant proposals. Knowing the implicit and multiple social rules by which these genres work, as well as knowing to some extent the social situations within which they are meaningfully used, is crucial for communicative competence in these fields. Genres are not fixed entities; on the contrary, as Prior (1995) suggests, "goals structuring generic activity need to be viewed as multiple rather than unified, varying with time, place and participants" (p. 55). Neither does a straightforward, one-to-one relationship connect genre, author, and TC; on the contrary, as figure 3.1 indicates, these terms overlap and each contributes to the overall context within which the others are to be understood.

The concept of thought collectives is integral to our discussion of genres because both genres and TCs belong to, and to some extent determine, each other's domain. A TC is very much a social structure (Giddens, 1979), with its own built-in system of rules and (social) practices. As Giddens notes, the "structural properties of social systems are both the medium and the outcome of practices that constitute those systems" (1979, p. 69); that is, there is a duality built into any TC, whereby what glues the collective together is also a result of the collective. The potential L2 writing instructor/author, then—very much a part of both the collective and the production of the text—forms and is formed by the text and the TC. To understand better how this is possible and what the ramifications are, it is necessary to address the related term *discourse community*. Although I touched briefly in my Introduction on Swales's (1990) criteria for discourse communities, I want to examine these criteria in greater depth here because I believe they apply equally to TCs: not only does each of these features hold genres in place, but each can be seen to enhance the professional/disciplinary cognitions of its participants. I have substituted the term *TC* for Swales's *discourse community*:

1. A TC has a broadly agreed-upon set of common public goals.
2. A TC has mechanisms for intercommunication among its members.
3. A TC uses its participatory mechanisms primarily to provide information and feedback.
4. A TC utilizes and hence possesses one or more genres in the communicative furtherance of its aims.
5. In addition to owning genres, a TC has acquired some specific lexis.
6. A TC has a threshold level of members with suitable degrees of relevant content and discoursal expertise. (p. 28)

Although Swales himself has since questioned whether his criteria are too strict,[1] I believe they are quite valuable, especially if we view them in terms of disciplinary orientations. One contribution is that they provide a baseline template from which to begin talking about genres. They also allow us to begin to conceptualize disciplinary TCs as subcultures that have relatively systematic, albeit generally implicit, rules regarding membership, goals, participation, and patterns of communication. As Robert Kaplan and I have pointed out elsewhere (Ramanathan and Kaplan, 1996a, 1996b), the implicit rules and social practices in (disciplinary) cultures and subcultures—-regarding, among other things, what is to be said, who is to speak, how it is to be said/presented, in other words, the selective nature of these rules—partially contribute to stabilizing genres.

Each of these criteria can be interpreted in this light. Regarding the first—that TCs have common goals—meaningful and structurally stable texts emerge largely from communities held together by shared goals and values. Certain textual forms become, in many ways, the vehicles through which the community's problems get addressed and its goals achieved. These texts emerge in response to the particular demands and needs of a community; "they are constructed for specific purposes by speakers and writers, and they always embody sets of generic conventions" (Kamberelis, 1995, p. 122). One general goal of the TESOL TC, for example, is to produce competent, self-reflective teachers of English. The genres and texts built into the social practices of the typical MA-TESOL degree—especially in relation to the development of potential L2 teachers—have arisen partially to address this need. Having student teachers write critical evaluations of a videotape of themselves teaching or having them write peer teaching observation reports are instances of practices that perpetuate the use of these textual forms and contribute to the development of students in their role as teachers.[2] Because these selective genres have over time proved relatively successful in achieving these TC goals—inasmuch as they partially contribute to producing critical, self-reflective teachers/authors—they have to some extent become stabilized.

Other stabilizing conventions related to achieving a TC's goals include ways the collective uses certain selective citing conventions. These conventions, to some extent, imply consensus regarding how research is to be reported and how references to connected works are to be made. "If citations are signals, then it is important that a citational semaphore is worked out to prevent messages from becoming confused" (Cronin, 1981, p. 21). The scientific community, for instance, which places a high premium on the replicability of results (of experiments, for example), has formalized conventions and rules for reporting research results that ensure against unnecessary duplication and the propagation of error (Cronin, 1981, p. 20). Giving such importance to (selective) citation conventions informs the applied linguistics/TESOL TCs as well: citing in these communities partially serves the function of contextualizing research in an existing body of work; citing the work of other people in particular ways in this chapter, for instance, indirectly ensures that certain rules are followed in its writing, thus contributing, albeit in minuscule ways, to stabilizing the genre of an academic essay. Encouraging potential L2 teachers to reflect on ways in which the writing assignments they are expected to fulfill and the citation practices they are expected to follow have direct consequences in terms of stabilizing genres in their discourse community will help them see connections between themselves and the larger community's goals.

The second and fifth criteria—that a TC has mechanisms for intercommunication between its members and that each TC develops its own lexis—also help to explain how genres stabilize. Members of a TC who become insiders of the community, partially out of longstanding participation in it, evolve a selective lexis—modes of communication, acronyms, jargon, textual forms—that facilitates easy communication among peers. The name TESOL is itself an acronym that has evolved partially because the community has its own lexis. It indexes a range of things to a peer but means very little, if anything, to an outsider. Among other things, it signals interest in other cultures, other peoples, other lifestyles, the general globalization of English, attitudes toward language learning and teaching, and oral and written communicative practices of groups of people. Even a subdomain—second-language writing—indexes a range of exclusionary points of interest and debates: process approaches to writing, critical thinking, holistic grading, and English proficiency placement exams, to name a few. All of these notions are embedded in and recast through particular social practices: classroom discussions, readings, office visits, chats in hallways, oral presentations, brief written responses to readings, term papers, data gathering.

Also, ordinary nontechnical words become part of a discourse community's lexicon (or "speak"). The term *socialization* can index, for an insider of the applied linguistics community, specific research domains: research in child language socialization practices (see, e.g., Heath, 1983; Ochs, 1988) or socialization research at tertiary levels of education, among other things. Practices such as these—the use of jargon terms, acronyms, what Giddens (1979) refers to as "reproduced relations"—contribute to constituting entire discourses (Gee, 1990) that, through constant use and reification, hold particular textual forms, genres, and lexicons in place. Ensuring that L2 instructors have some meta-awareness of how the selective parlance they are being socialized into helps to sustain the intercommunication between the collective's members and to stabilize the community's lexis will afford them a clearer sense of their role and position in the larger community.

Using participatory mechanisms to provide information and feedback (#3) as well as using one or more genres to communicate aims (#4) seem to be yet more ways in which TCs reinforce the use of particular genres. Returning to the applied linguistics/TESOL examples, both collectives use particular textual forms when disseminating communal information to their members— for example, membership forms, reminders for payments, calls for abstracts. The collectives offer insiders feedback about decisions made and votes passed by their respective executive boards, as well as editorials on the current state of affairs in the discourse community. Frequently, written and publicly acknowledged pieces validate the textual forms in which they emerge—letters to the editor, information about upcoming conferences—and exclude a whole range of other forms—food recipes or ideas for sewing, for instance. Thus, L2 writing instructors need to be cognizant that the shared goals of this community constrain not just the content of what is disseminated but the forms through which dissemination occurs.[3] Making L2 writing teachers aware of how the genres they are acquiring and teaching are selective, privileged ones that have become this way because they have gotten reproduced through the community's social practices (because these genres work well given the community's goals) will heighten the writing teachers' awareness of how certain textual forms get selected and reproduced over others. It will engender in L2 writing teachers a sense in which they can contribute toward shaping social practices so as to eventually allow other potentially useful textual forms to enter the community.

Last, genre stability is partially maintained by the experts in any disciplinary discourse community (#6), thereby contributing to the collective's structuring process. The relatively fully developed nature of the experts' disciplinary persona exerts influence on what may be said and how, thus contributing to conditions that govern the stability and reproduction of certain systems.

These experts have reached wide audiences through their publications and research, their opinions and views serve as authoritative sources, and they have produced some of the key touchstones of the community. Some examples might include Heath's and Ochs's work on language socialization, Kaplan's research in contrastive rhetoric, Labov's analysis of the narrative, Swales's work on genres, and Tannen's work in discourse analysis. All of these individuals have had longstanding influence on the field. Their works serve as templates on which the rest of the community builds, and their thoughts are embodied in specific textual forms particular to academic writing. Kaplan's (1966) controversial "doodles" article would not have fueled research in contrastive rhetoric had he written it in the form of a memo, for instance. For one thing, *Language Learning* would not have accepted it for publication.

People who review abstracts for conferences can also be seen to fill the role of experts inasmuch as they, partially on the basis of their developed social (disciplinary) consciousness, police the general form of submitted abstracts, for which the requirements undoubtedly vary from disciplinary community to community. In their study of 294 abstracts submitted to the 1992–1993 conference of the American Association of Applied Linguistics, Kaplan and colleagues (1994) identified several rhetorical and pragmatic features that went into successful abstracts (i.e., those that got accepted for presentation). Given that each abstract is typically read by at least two or three readers, mutual consensus on a successful abstract strongly implies that the abstract meets the discourse expectations of readers; both in terms of content and form the text is appropriate. "Because genres are rhetorical and pragmatic in principle and practice, understanding their forms and functions requires an awareness of domain epistemologies and content knowledge, possible and relevant intertextual links, specific situations of text-making practice, and abiding reception practices" (Kamberelis, 1995, p. 145). These practices show the importance of meeting the discourse/genre expectations of a community of readers who bring their generic expectations (Coe,

1994) of what a well-written abstract in their discipline is to their reading of one, and on this basis they regulate what does or does not pass as a successful abstract.

It would appear, then, that TCs, authors, and genres coproduce each other; each mutually sustains the stability of the other in a symbiotic relationship. Genres that evolve from particular disciplinary collectives reflect, to some extent, the culture of the collective (Becher, 1981), including the way in which the collective perceives and addresses problems in its fields (MacDonald, 1987). Each discipline and each author in the discipline not only controls what issues are defined as problems and how they get addressed but also helps develop, stabilize, and reinforce particular textual forms by which to confront these problems. All of these are issues about which L2 writing instructors need meta-awareness because they are genre related and thus, by extension, writing related.

Genres, TCs, and Dynamism

Genres are also dynamic, however. As Berkenkotter and Huckin (1993) put it, "Genres must do more than encapsulate intersubjective perceptions of recurring situations" (p. 481). They reflect changing sociocultural and political realities and thus have components of flexibility built into them. The following points attempt to capture some ways that genres change. These points do not aim to be comprehensive but rather to serve as starting points from which to talk about how TCs change incrementally. Disciplinary communities other than applied linguistics/TESOL are employed as examples because the applied linguistics and TESOL TCs are not old enough to have generated obvious genre changes, as have communities such as anthropology, science, or business. Sensitizing L2 writing instructors to each of these points will, I believe, enable them to regard genres not as fixed, unchanging entities about which they (or anybody else) can do nothing but as structures that evolve to accommodate the growing/changing needs of communities of which they are a part.

Genres evolve and change to meet the growing and changing sociocognitive needs of TCs. Genre changes are partially visible through the kind of internal dynamism found in Huckin's (1987) study of 350 scientific journal articles, reflecting the changing needs of the scientific discourse community. Based on his analysis of formal textual patterns, Huckin found significant changes in the way scientific articles organize their information, especially in the way experimental results are foregrounded in titles, abstracts, and introductions, with methods and procedures sections being given less importance. His interviews with scientists revealed that one important reason for these changes arose because readers are less able to keep up with current research and generally skim through articles to pick up salient points. Because these scientist-readers are also writers, their individual reading behavior affects their writing strategies. Inasmuch as they also belong to a scientific community, they find themselves responding in similar ways to similar communicative pressures. Likewise, Atkinson (1998b), in his historical study of the *Philosophical Transactions of the Royal Society of London,* has shown how changes in scientific paradigms between 1675 and 1975 necessitated gradual change in that rhetorical structure. Thus, genres evolve to meet needs both at the communal level of the discourse community at large and at the individual level of particular scientist-writers. Potential L2 teachers need to be aware of this point, if only to see how both the individual and the community influence textual forms.

Genres evolve to meet the needs of changing technology. The adaptations of different TCs to technological advancements also contribute to the changing nature of text types. Yates and Orlikowski (1992) studied ways that business correspondence changes in relation to technological changes. Their study included an examination of the differences between a business letter (a form of external, public communication) and a memo (a form of internal, relatively private communication). They maintain that the basic format of these two types of communication remained the same in the 1800s. Because organizations were smaller, relatively little internal communication was needed and the traditional business letter worked just as well as the memo to meet all the needs. However, as businesses expanded and typewriters were introduced, textual changes such as underlining, using all capital letters, and using subheadings gradually emerged. Tab stops contributed to making columnar formats easier, and gradually this type of formatting became a regular feature of internal correspondence. It is from such formatting that the *To/From/Subject/Date* headings of a memo evolved.

Another instance of genres evolving to meet the needs of technological advancements arises from the current extensive use of electronic mail, which has created a whole new subgenre of the letter. Correspondents do not typically put their address at the top of the e-mail letter, nor do they—unless they are being extremely formal—put the address of the receiver. Correspondents do not generally note the date because most e-mail systems automatically indicate when the message was sent. Although these points about e-mail do not necessarily address issues in particular academic disciplines, they are relevant because they deal with how one particular force—namely technological advancement—contributes to textual changes across numerous academic TCs and influences both genres and authors (Hunt, 1994).[4]

Genres adapt to changes in ideology and worldviews in TCs. As ideologies and worldviews in TCs change—partially with the furthering of research in particular domains or with the current interdisciplinary nature of many disciplines—textual practices are likely to change. Current anthropology, for instance, influenced as it has been by poststructuralist thought, has seen fairly drastic changes in textual practices. Marcus and Fisher (1986) maintain that the recent critical examination of the rhetoric of anthropology has called into question the validity of traditional ethnographies. Because the ethnographer's account of a culture is now perceived as falsely coherent (given that cultures, according to Marcus and Fisher, are not internally coherent but are full of contradictions) and as a "construction" (that has evolved out of the ethnographer's own social consciousness and is not really reflective of the culture under study), new ways of accurately representing cultures have developed. The use of the first person, for instance, is becoming increasingly widespread, as is a style of writing that represents the internal contradictions of a culture. Such changes in genres and textual forms have occurred because the disciplines' and the authors' prevailing social consciousness—general ideologies and values—have been called into question and have, in some instances, begun to change. Reflection on these issues will allow (L1 and) L2 teachers to recognize connections between the textual forms with which they work and the prevailing ideologies of their disciplines (as opposed to just accepting these forms at face value and not seeing them as embedded in and emerging from distinct disciplinary worldviews).

Genres change as individual writers take liberties with textual conventions. Some disciplinary communities, such as creative writing, often encourage license with textual forms, whereas others, such as applied linguistics, are likely to frown on it. Rather than seeing genres and textual structures as constraining the individual writer, Fowler (1982, p. 31) maintains that in some ways genres provide room for textual experimentation:

> [Genres] offer room, one might say, for [the author] to write in—a habitation of mediated definiteness; a propositional neutral space; a literary matrix by which to order his experience during composition. . . . Instead of a daunting void, they extend a provocatively definite invitation. The writer is invited to match experience and form in a specific yet undetermined way. Accepting the invitation does not solve his problems of expression. . . . But it gives him access to formal ideas as to how a variety of constituents might be suitably combined.

Well-established scholars in disciplines that are generally traditional in their use of text types seem to have greater freedom in breaking with genre conventions. Stephen Jay Gould, for instance, challenges the way science—particularly biology—gets written, and in his own writing he blurs boundaries between "narrative and exposition, science and history, research activity and research finding" (Kamberelis, 1995, p. 137).[5] Individual writers in different disciplinary communities may motivate genre changes by producing texts that are structured differently from the norm (sometimes to reflect their feelings and views). It is partially through such creative efforts that individual writers create newer "textual spaces"; it is through such creations that existing social expectations and practices get challenged, questioned, and in some cases, eventually recast. Recent research in sociolinguistics (e.g., Ramanathan, 1997), following current trends in anthropology, has attempted to combine a personal style and an active voice with empirical research, which in the past might not have been acceptable.

Genre Sensitizing in L2 Writing Instructors: Why?

Although genre awareness does not by any means constitute an overall panacea to potential issues and/or problems in the socialization process, it can provide access into developing the meta-knowledge of our graduate students and, more specifically, of our L2 writing instructors. As Fairclough points out, education at its best is "a site of reflection upon and analysis of the sociolinguistic order and the order of discourse, and in so far as educational institutions equip learners with a critical language awareness, they equip them with a resource for intervention in and reshaping of discursive practices and the power relations that ground them, both in other domains and within education itself" (Fairclough, 1995, p. 217).

Engaging applied linguistics and TESOL graduate students in critical dialogue about the sociotextual practices of their TCs will afford them insight into the discipline's ideological practices, which "people draw upon without thinking" and which often "embody assumptions which directly or indirectly legitimize existing [textual/generic] conventions" (Fairclough, 1989, p. 33).

Such reflection will, as the above quote points out, provide them with a critical language awareness that will encourage them to question the ways in which they, through their involvement in their TCs, are shaped by disciplinary social practices and how as contributors to the TESOL community they help shape those practices in turn. Such awareness on their part will lead them to rethink discursive conventions in a variety of realms and to (in ideal circumstances) generate a sense of empowerment that will allow them to make necessary changes. The following are some implications of this heightened consciousness.

Connecting the trees with the forest. L2 writing instructors need to be aware of the ways that everyday disciplinary activities in which they participate—such as having ESL students write in their journals or write responses to particular readings—are, partially at least, genre-producing social activities that ultimately contribute to binding a whole TC together. Such understanding will better enable them to see how relatively minute social activities help achieve the overall goals of the discourse community. Acknowledging how the practice of writing abstracts for term papers or conferences stabilizes the abstract as a textual form in the larger community is a step in this direction. Likewise, heightening awareness of how peer reviewing in writing classrooms is a social practice that partially keeps the genre of the academic essay in place will allow L2 writing instructors to contextualize smaller classroom activities within larger community goals.

Providing opportunities for L2 writing TAs to explain or talk about—to engage in metatalk, in other words—connections they see between their classroom practices and the larger community's goals will encourage them to reflect on some of the very practices in which they are gaining expertise. Having them articulate various sociotextual links in the practices they participate in, establish, and keep in place will foster in them a clearer sense of their contribution to the larger disciplinary constellation. Too often (potential) writing instructors get caught up in the minutiae of class activities and lose sight of how their social practices in their individual programs, as well as those they encourage in

their writing classrooms, are directly connected to the stabiliza-
tion (and potential destabilization) of genres in the community of
which they are a part.

*Making L2 writing instructors aware of the need to pass on genre
awareness to their students.* Once L2 writing TAs are sensitized to
sociotextual conventions (for instance, in the applied linguistics
community) and ways that particular social practices reinforce
and validate the use of certain textual forms over other "occluded"
forms (Swales, 1998) in the community, they will have a better
sense of the relative power associated with the mastery of certain
genres and the larger disciplinary goals such mastery is able to
achieve. Inculcating this sense of how value, and thus power, gets
unevenly distributed across text types is worthwhile because it
will make them more sensitive to the genre needs of *their* students. Genre knowledge is especially important given that much
recent research in education has pointed out ways that minority
and L2 students are disadvantaged because genres are not explicitly taught (Cope and Kalantzis, 1993; Delpit, 1988).

The problems, of course, differ somewhat between indigenous
minority students, on the one hand, and recent immigrants,
refugees, and foreign students, on the other. Each group comes
equipped, however, with a variety of genre-based assumptions
acquired through socialization and teaching that are sometimes
inappropriate in the context of formal school settings and, more
important, in the context of academic disciplinary writing.
Speakers of black vernacular English (BVE) or of Mexican-
American nonstandard English (MANSE) or of any of the wide
variety of nonstandard forms employed typically in the United
States have been demonstrated to be disadvantaged in terms of the
acquisition of more traditional academic genres.

Recent arrivals in the United States, receiving perhaps their
first exposure to the culture at large, let alone to the academic
culture, also find themselves disadvantaged; some (e.g., visa students) bring with them well-established notions of academic genres that prove to be inappropriate in their new setting (see, e.g.,
Fox, 1994). The extreme approach to teaching writing adopted in

several schools across the United States, where (overt) teaching of genres and textual forms is downplayed has been said to disadvantage black students (Delpit, 1988); components of the extreme version of the process approach draw directly from socialization practices that white middle-class children generally have access to and that lower-class black children or children from other cultural backgrounds do not. Making instruction at least partially genre sensitive is one way to ensure that all learners at all levels of schooling, regardless of background, have relatively equal access to school-based literacy (at least as far as learning in the classroom is concerned).

Helping potential (L1 and) L2 writing instructors develop their disciplinary selves. Encouraging L2 writing TAs to engage in metatalk on how the discipline's social practices contribute to their evolving mastery over particular textual forms and, by extension, their disciplinary personas would also help them to become fuller participants in their own discourse community. Christie (1993) talks about the importance of enabling all students to acquire the two registers—the pedagogical register and the content register—that make up the curriculum genre. The pedagogical register "structures and gives purpose to the teaching-learning activity so that students can proceed to dealing with content"; the content register has to do with the subject matter dealt with "in pursuit of pedagogical goals" (p. 155); the former register is concerned "primarily with teaching how to write," the latter with the "content for writing" (p. 158). In successful instances students should be able to manipulate both registers effectively. Although Christie discusses these issues in relation to using genres when teaching children, her points apply for L2 writing teachers as well.

Getting L2 writing instructors in applied linguistics/TESOL departments to recognize at the outset that in order to get their MA and PhD degrees they need to have mastered both registers—that they need to know not just content but particular textual forms including term papers, research proposals, presentations, and research papers—will eventually make them better teachers. Although MA and doctoral programs do this in general—inasmuch as students by being apprenticed to particular professors and advisers pick up both kinds of registers—heightening student awareness to the process so that they can make conscious connections between the social practices they are engaged in and the general evolution of their disciplinary selves will empower them as writers, readers, and researchers. Having them engage in metatalk at the end of the first or second year in the program, wherein they trace the growth in their disciplinary selves from the time they entered the program to the current moment, is one concrete way of achieving this goal. Making them metacognitively aware of how their gradual mastery over particular textual forms—a mastery that emerges as much from their teaching of certain forms as from their using some of these forms themselves—plays a significant role in their individual growth, while contributing to keeping certain textual forms stable in the community, will enhance their ability to locate themselves in both micro- and macro-level disciplinary practices. Such multidimensional awareness will allow them to take critical stances toward themselves as teachers and researchers.

The socialization that novice L2 writing teachers go through in their immersion in a disciplinary community eventually influences, at least indirectly, whether genres (and eventually TCs) stabilize or change. As students begin to move easily in and out of linguistically configured situations, they recognize connections among particular forms, identities, relationships, actions, and stances (Ochs, Schegloff, and Thompson, 1996). Heightening their awareness of the socializing process, making them metacognitively aware of their own location in relation to genres, TCs, and their L2 students, will contribute to their understanding of their profession and their role within their TCs. Students of writing must know that their production is realized in actual TCs; teachers of writing need to recognize that both their own discourses and the discourses they try to inculcate among learners are rooted in actual TCs. Sensitivity to the function of genres may expedite the realization of this rootedness.

Chapter 4

The Politics of Written Knowledge

A major pitfall of research in the sociology of curriculum has been its willingness to accept text form as a mere adjunct means for the delivery of ideological content: the former described in terms of dominant metaphors, images, or key ideas; the latter described in terms of the sum total of values, beliefs, and ideas which might be seen to constitute a false consciousness. For much content analysis presumes that text mirrors or reflects a particular ideological position, which in turn can be connected to special class interests. . . . It is predicated on the possibility of a one-to-one identification of school knowledge with textually represented ideas of the dominant classes. Even those critics who have recognized that the ideology encoded in curricular texts may reflect the internally contradictory character of a dominant culture have tended to neglect the need for a more complex model of text analysis, one that does not suppose that texts are simply readable, literal representations of "someone else's" version of social reality, objective knowledge and human relations. For texts do not always mean or communicate what they say.

—Allan Luke, *Literacy, Textbooks, and Ideology*

This chapter is devoted to partially addressing the politics of how the TC's conceptions of appropriate writing and written knowledge get displayed, reproduced, and reified in college-level writing textbooks and the general importance of sensitizing graduating TESOLers to uncovering latent assumptions in materials they use and the profession/larger TC produces. Textbooks are inherently ideological tools, both progressive and retrogressive, depending on social context. They "can be fought because they are a part of a system of moral regulation. They can be championed both as providing essential assistance in the labor of teaching and as a part of a larger strategy of democratization" (Apple and Christian-Smith, 1991, p. 8). The roles that textbooks play and the sociocultural practices they embody are crucial for all of us ESL professionals to uncover to better understand not only the internal qualities of a textbook (its content and layout) but the politics of how and by whom textbooks are used.

All of the points regarding writing textbooks address sociocultural implications that potential L2 teachers need to recognize and question. Writing in appropriate forms and displaying particular writing skills in their TCs—both in individual programs and the larger discipline/s—are validated, reinforced, and sustained by a range of social practices and preferences (see chapter 3). It is crucial for L2 teachers-in-training to turn the reflective and critical lens on themselves and their profession to begin to see how they, through their teaching and adoption of particular (sometimes problematic) materials, assume culturally embedded stances that may inhibit them from recognizing that their L2 students bring equally valued ways of organizing information. Although inappropriate in the new culture, these practices are relevant and necessary in the students' respective home backgrounds.

I do need to add here that my presentation of these problematic points regarding North American, middle-class, college-level literacy is not intended to be monolithic or static; neither is it intended to essentialize or simplify the writing requirements our students are expected to meet. Instead, the discussion is aimed at encouraging TESOLers to recognize that their "commonsensical," "natural" ways of organizing information are based on culturally valued social practices. This is not to say that local and subcultural differences within communities in this culture do not exist, nor is it to deny that North American culture, like most cultures today, is more or less a hybrid culture with relatively intense zones of contact with other cultures. My point is that in spite of these differences and interactions, certain overarching ways of being (including thinking, feeling, writing, believing, dressing) prevail—tendencies that allow us to recognize cultural differences when we see or experience them. Unfortunately, the discursive act of writing about culture or cultural ways automatically runs the risk of seeming reductive. It is precisely because culture and cultural issues are difficult concepts, however, that TESOLers need to be engaged in debates about how to think and write about them, without their becoming overdetermining categories. By openly acknowledging and voicing the difficulty of writing about these murky terrains, I hope to stave off possible misinterpretations.

The textbooks I examine in this chapter are writing-related texts that potential and experienced L2 teachers frequently use in their ESL writing classes. Many graduating TESOLers find themselves teaching various levels of writing in tertiary contexts (community colleges, language institutes, four-year schools) to college-bound ESL students and end up adopting a range of texts—often written for L1 audiences—in their L2 classrooms; hence the need to encourage their meta-awareness about teaching materials they might use or consider using.

There seem to be at least three issues pertinent to the critical questioning of textbooks dealing with writing: (1) the extent to which these materials actually enable students to become better writers in English, (2) ways in which textbooks advocate how written knowledge is to be displayed, and (3) latent sociocultural leanings in what gets stressed and promoted as crucial to effective writing. Uncovering implications in these issues will enable TESOLers to begin thinking about how culturally embedded their own and the discipline's teaching and learning practices are, thus fostering in them a degree of cross-cultural astuteness.

I address three rhetorical terms commonly used in writing textbooks—*critical thinking, audience,* and *voice*—to demonstrate how taken-for-granted notions can be uncovered. I do not by any means claim that these interpretations are correct; on the contrary, they are only one of several possible ways of critically reading pedagogical materials. Neither am I claiming that critical thinking should not be taught. What I am challenging are textbook presentations of terms such as the above. I wish to under-score the importance of the general exercise itself: picking out common, everyday terms and questioning the bases on which they are built. I begin by addressing how these words (and texts) are partially situated and defined in terms of the sociocognitive practices of the TCs of which they are a part.

Critical Thinking, Audience, and Voice as Embedded in Sociocognitive Practices

The emphasis placed on developing thinking skills across various levels of educational curricula (Ennis, 1962, 1987; Norris, 1985; Walton, 1993) in which students are encouraged to write for an audience and to project a strong voice seems to reflect a general view that this practice is largely cognitive. As I pointed out in chapter 1, however, research in situated cognition (Brown, Collins, and Duguid, 1989; Lave and Wenger, 1991) challenges the idea that the social and the cognitive can be studied independently, argu-ing that the social context in which the cognitive activity takes place is an integral part of that activity, not just the surrounding context for it (Resnick, 1990, p. 4). As Lave (1988) and Goody (1989) argue, our definition of the cognitive is influenced by assumptions that derive from social and economic arrangements with long, his-torical roots.

From this point of view, a social practice such as critical think-ing (Atkinson, 1998a)—including the ability to effectively gauge the audience and assume an appropriate voice—is not only a cog-nitive practice but a sociocognitive one whose detailed workings are hidden from our view because it has become a practice that we take for granted. This practice is mediated—as is any prac-tice—on both social and individual planes by a TC's tools and signs, which reinforce and sustain it. Two critical corollary points regarding such signs must be taken into account when attempt-ing to understand Vygotsky's explanation of human mental func-tioning. The first is that "[by] their nature, signs [tools] are social, not organic or individual" (Vygotsky, 1981, p. 137); they are prod-

ucts of sociocultural evolution and are therefore inherently positioned in sociocultural contexts. They are not invented by the
individual or discovered in the individual's independent interaction with nature, and they are not inherited in the form of "innate
predispositions" (Wertsch, 1991, p. 92); instead, by being a part
of a sociocultural milieu, individuals appropriate these media-
tional tools (Leont'ev, 1959). The ability to think critically about
the audience and to project an appropriate voice to that audience
can be seen to be rooted as much, if not more, in social contexts
as in the individual. The second relevant Vygotskian point is that
"[by] being included in the process of behaviour, the . . . tool [text-
books] alters the entire flow and structure of mental functions"
(Vygotsky, 1981, p. 137). In other words, the tools aid in transformations—including social and cognitive ones—that occur when
the learner is being inducted into the practices of the TC.

These points have important implications for the present discussion. Given that tools themselves are sociocultural in nature,
and given that they mediate between the social practice and
learner, it follows that people of shared sociocultural backgrounds
have a relatively easier time accessing and/or communicating with
those tools. Ethnographic research on literacy practices has shown
us that middle-class socialization procedures such as reading bed-
time stories at home (Heath, 1983) or participating in show-and-
tell in school (Michaels, 1981) ultimately prepare children for
essayist/school-based literacy. In the light of the present discussion, tools that are typically used to teach college-level ESL students are drawn, by and large, from materials and social practices
in the L1 world that mandate very specific ways in which written
knowledge is to be displayed. Enrolled TESOLers need to be aware
of these routines as they teach their L2 classes.

Critical Thinking vs. Critical Pedagogy

The surplus of materials—programs, textbooks, appraisal kits—
devoted to critical thinking (CT) over the last decade points
partially to how problematic this notion has become in education-

related circles. Although I do not question the appropriateness of teaching *all* our students to be critical thinkers—indeed this entire book calls for encouraging student teachers to be critical—I wonder about the divergent meanings of the phrase and the narrow and problematic ways in which the term is presented in and taught through undergraduate composition textbooks. Before I address its pervasive influence in a range of school-related areas, I would like to discuss briefly some ways in which the phrase (as used in composition textbooks) differs from a related phrase, critical pedagogy (CP). Canagarajah (2001) offers the following valuable breakdown:

Critical Thinking	Critical Pedagogy
monological thinking	dialogical thinking
asocial/mentalistic	socially grounded
objective/instrumental	self-reflexive
dispassionate	ethical
neutral	politically engaged
rationalistic	multimodal
universal/transcendental	context-bound
leads to understanding	leads to change

As Canagarajah's list points out, CP seems to flesh out aspects of CT. CP is dialogical, self-reflexive, politically engaged, and oriented toward constructive change. CT, in contrast, at least as presented in the Li composition textbooks and as Canagarajah depicts, is limited. Although like CP it encourages cross-questioning from multiple perspectives, it remains a mentalistic, rational, dispassionate activity that leads to understanding but not necessarily to social change. Indeed, many composition textbooks claiming to teach CT demonstrate to varying degrees some or all of the qualities listed under CT above—qualities that are problematic for nonnative speakers of English.

The General Pervasiveness of Critical Thinking

National appraisals on the state of education belittle rote memory and cry out for the inclusion of thinking/reasoning skills in curricula as the fourth R (Siegal, 1990). The Carnegie Task Force on Teaching as a Profession (1986) and the Holmes Group (1986) stress the importance of teaching thinking skills to both students and teachers. The Commission on the Humanities (1980), the College Board (1983), and the National Educational Association (Futrell, 1987) similarly promote the incorporation of teaching thinking skills in current curricula; many mainstream universities in the United States require their students to take CT courses. There is much debate not only over what the phrase means and how to define it (Ennis, 1962; Glaser, 1984; McPeck, 1981, 1990) but also over educational levels at which it should be implemented and how it can best be tested and assessed. This chapter enters the debate not to offer one more definition of *critical thinking* (for comprehensive discussions of the term, see Ennis, 1981, 1987; Johnson, 1992; McPeck, 1981; Nelson, 1981; Nickerson, 1984, 1987; Norris, 1985; Paul, 1985) or to suggest ways in which it can be evaluated. Rather I want to examine some aspects of a specific set of textbooks that purport to foster these skills, and I want to explore some implications of these materials for a specific student population.

The pedagogical artifacts under consideration are rhetorically oriented freshman composition (FC) textbooks. The readings in these texts are predicated on the view that students should be encouraged to examine critically and to question the social world they inhabit (Bizzell, 1992; Shor, 1993). Thus, most of these readings revolve around current sociopolitical problems such as animal rights, censorship, or the right to die (see appendix B for a partial selection of topics covered) to encourage students to examine critically certain cultural "givens." Accompanying these readings are rhetorical conduits, or heuristics, by which some of these social problems can be addressed. Popular as these textbooks are, both the readings and the conduits accompanying them are based on problematic assumptions particularly disadvantageous to L2 student writers. The heuristics and readings I examine revolve around at least three related conduits that these textbooks identify as central to the development of critical thinking/writing skills:

1. Developing students' sense of informal logic toward strengthening their reasoning strategies
2. Developing and refining problem-solving skills
3. Developing the ability to look for hidden assumptions and fallacies in arguments

All three of these features are identified as central in the five standardized (machine-gradable) English-language critical thinking tests (administered to high school students) currently available on the North American continent. These tests are:

1. *Cornell Critical Thinking Test, Level X* (Ennis and Millman, 1985a)
2. *Cornell Critical Thinking Test, Level Z* (Ennis and Millman, 1985b)
3. *New Jersey Test of Reasoning Skills* (Shipman, 1983)
4. *Ross Test of Higher Cognitive Processes* (Ross and Ross, 1976)
5. Watson-Glaser Critical Thinking Appraisal (Watson and Glaser, 1980)

The three related conduits are in themselves problematic, with serious implications when transferred into advanced college L2 writing classrooms because they draw on shared cultural knowledge that the L2 learner may not have. L2 composition students are doubly disadvantaged: not only do they have to grapple with U.S.-specific social problems, but they must also deal with tools that are in themselves problematic. Difficulties such as the ones I examine here, as well as those I have discussed elsewhere (Ramanathan and Kaplan, 1996a), lead to questioning whether the teaching of writing might be more effective for both L1 and L2 student writers if it were taught within more situated contexts

(Brown et al., 1989; Collins, 1991) such as specific disciplines. Anchoring writing in a discipline will provide students with a specific context (Bizzell, 1992; Brannon, 1995; Petraglia, 1995; Swales, 1990; Young, 1994) within which to gauge what constitutes problematic issues; it will also give them a clearer sense of discipline-specific rhetorical tools with which to address those issues. I touch on this issue toward the end of this chapter.

Critical Thinking and Freshman Composition Textbooks: How We Got Here

To provide at least a partial backdrop against which to place CT in freshman composition (FC), I partially reconstruct the background from which this concept emerged and briefly address CT as a sociocognitive practice. I then discuss the problematic nature of the three common features that all of the examined composition texts identify as central to critical thinking. Where relevant, this section also discusses the implications of these assumptions for nonnative student writers.

According to Kennedy, Fisher, and Ennis (1991), part of the critical thinking debate focuses on whether critical thinking is the same across disciplines or whether all critical thinking abilities are specific to disciplines. At one end of the spectrum are thinkers such as Glaser (1984) and McPeck (1981), who uphold a subject-specific view of critical thinking; Project IMPACT (Winocur, 1985) in California, for instance, attempted to integrate thinking instruction into content areas, as well as math, reading, and the language arts, at the middle and high school levels (cf. Kennedy et al., 1991). At the other extreme are proponents who advocate instrumental enrichment (Fuerstein, Jensen, Hoffman, and Rand, 1985), "lateral thinking" (deBono, 1983), and "structure of the intellect" (Meeker, 1969). These experts advocate separate thinking courses and programs such as Philosophy for Children (Lipman, 1982). Ennis (1985) and Sternberg (1987) point out that each approach has its advantages and have put forward a mixed model (Sternberg, 1987, p. 225) that integrates elements of each.

Current L1 composition textbooks appear to fall toward the end of the spectrum that advocates separate discipline-free thinking skills. The nature of topics in current rhetoric-oriented FC texts seems to reflect strong ties to a currently fashionable movement in education, namely critical/radical pedagogy (Shor, 1993; Shor and Freire, 1987). Much of this movement is centered on the idea that schools should serve as "sites for learning about the principles of critical literacy and democracy" because such education would promote the development of "critical citizenship, civic courage, and . . . organic intellectuals" (Aronowitz and Giroux, 1985, p. 216). This movement aims to achieve its ideas by stressing forms of learning and knowledge that will provide a critical understanding of how social reality works, of how certain "disparities between democratic principles and undemocratic realities" (Benesch, 1993, p. 546) are sustained and reinforced, and of how those aspects related to the logic of domination can be changed.

The above pedagogy follows closely on the heels of liberal humanism, a movement in the 1960s that stressed the importance of empowering students and parents and of connecting school to students' real lives (Benesch, 2001). This movement—frequently associated with John Dewey—emerged primarily as a response to a conservative demand that schools offer more rigorous courses in math and science—a notion in keeping with the idea that mastery of techniques is equivalent to a "full" education. For Dewey the purpose of education was not so much to prepare students for jobs or skills but rather for the broad requirements of citizenship in a democratic society. Dewey also claimed that it was crucial for every child to participate in the learning experience as opposed to being a passive object of education, which was later echoed—albeit more vociferously—by radical pedagogue Paulo Freire (for a comprehensive history of composition, see Berlin, 1987).

Radical pedagogues adopted and extended yet another view of Dewey's: the idea that "knowledge is a perception of those connections of an object that determine its applicability in a given situation" (Dewey, 1966, p. 200). In other words, it was important for schools to teach students to apply their learning in the real world. Self-knowledge, Dewey believed, was the key to a person's knowledge of the world and specifically to the ability to connect contemporary experience to received information. This view— that schools devise curricula around information and the real world—informs both current views about critical thinking in general and FC texts in particular.

Although Dewey's movement became popular, it failed to become completely integrated into school ideology; instead, it was appropriated "piecemeal into a hybrid discourse" of liberal reform that has dominated U.S. schools since the turn of the 20th century (Aronowitz and Giroux, 1985, p. 7). Radical pedagogues believed that "although he [Dewey] had a clear idea of what schools ought to be, he carefully avoids making a social and political analysis of what schools are" (Aronowitz and Giroux, 1985, p. 9). Likewise, Gramsci (1971), the noted Italian Marxist, did not address what schools actually do; instead, his views primarily focused on developing a school form that would enable subaltern children not only to gain access to the dominant discourse (Gee, 1990) but to relate it critically to dimensions of their own histories, experiences, and cultures. Freire, on the other hand, did address social and political inequalities that school structures perpetuated. Like Dewey and Gramsci, he stressed the importance of validating oppressed voices (in his case Brazilian peasants) by connecting the individual to historical and contemporary circumstances. Education had to have the practical outcome of transforming society to meet the collective needs of individuals; it became for him the "central terrain where power and politics operate out of a dialectical relation between individuals and groups who live out their lives with specific historical conditions and structural constraints" (Aronowitz and Giroux, 1985, p. 12).

Many freshman composition programs aiming to develop critical thinking skills can be located against this partial background. Bizzell, a central figure in L1 composition theory, for instance, openly acknowledged her affiliation with Freire in her work (1992). Like Freire, she hoped to foster "critical consciousness" through literacy schooling, which in turn could be focused on inequities in the larger social order. However, she has since questioned the causal relation between critical consciousness and academic thinking and has, in fact, gone on record rejecting the imposition of academic discourse on all students at all costs. Other factors that have contributed to sensitizing students in writing courses to their political responsibilities, whether as leaders or simply as active participants (Berlin, 1987), have been the contributions of rhetoricians from a variety of fields, including poststructuralist literary and cultural criticism (Barthes, 1988; Eagleton, 1988; Lentricchia and McLaughlin, 1987; Said, 1988) and philosophical pragmatism (Rorty, 1995). Rhetoricians operating in this mode have tended to "move in the direction of the epistemic, regarding rhetoric principally as a *method of discovering*, and even *creating knowledge*, frequently within socially defined discourse communities" (Berlin, 1987, p. 183, my emphasis).

The idea of creating knowledge (which, as we saw in the Introduction, is crucial to creation and sustenance of TCs) seems to inform the readings in the textbooks under investigation. Even a cursory examination of topics covered in several current L1 composition texts points to the seriousness with which they view the importance of creating learners' knowledge by sensitizing them to contemporary public issues and the importance of enabling writers to take a stand on an issue. The texts are designed as aids to writing thoughtful, effective arguments on important political, social, scientific, ethical, and religious issues (see, e.g., Barnet and Bedau, 1993; 2002). Likewise, an examination of the rhetoric sections of these textbooks reveals an emphasis that regards rhetoric as a method of discovering through the development of "respectable techniques" (as opposed to "gimmicks") by which to target these public issues. Thus, both the readings and the rhetoric accompanying them point to the importance of teaching student writers how to order and make sense of the world, but as the present analysis attempts to underscore, much in this sense-making process deserves critical attention.

Induction into the CT practice for L2 student writers is a difficult process given that they come to the writing context having been socialized in their own, often very different, culturally valued practices (Connor and Kaplan, 1987). Students respond to writing tasks having been socialized into analyzing problems, with particular reasoning strategies (features associated with the CT practice discussed here) that are not only acceptable in their respective cultures but that are compatible with the linguistic means provided by their languages (Berman and Slobin, 1994). Kellerman (1995, pp. 138–139), citing Berman and Slobin's evidence, presents four versions of the same event interpreted in four different languages to illustrate the point that resources available to the speakers of different languages prompt different presentations of the event.

Below is a slightly abbreviated cross-language example showing how different languages filter the way in which events are related. It comes from transcripts of children with different native languages relating a story from a set of pictures without words (Berman and Slobin, 1994, p. 11). All of the children in these examples (their exact ages, including months, in parentheses) are native speakers of the respective languages:

English
And he starts running. And he tips him off over a cliff into the water. And he lands. (9:11)

German
Der Hirsch nahm den Jungen auf sein Geweih und schmiß ihm den Abhang hinunter genau ins Wasser. [The deer took the boy on his antlers and hurled him down from the cliff right into the water.] (9:11)

Spanish
El ciervo le llevo hasta un sitio, donde debajo habia un rio. Entonces el ciervo tiro perro y al nino at rio. Y despues, cayeron. [The deer took

him to a place, where below there was a river. Then the deer threw the dog and the boy to the river. And then they fell.] (9:8)

Hebrew
Ve ha' ayil nivhal, ve hu hixtil laruts. Ve hakelets rats axarav, ve higia lemcok she mixtaxat haya bista, ve hu astar, ve hayeled ve hakelev naflu labista beyaxad. [And the deer was startled, and he began to run. And the dog ran after him, and he reached the cliff that has a swamp underneath, and he stopped, and the boy and the dog fell into the swamp together.] (9:7)

Berman and Slobin claim that the differences among these excerpts are to some extent determined by the linguistic possibilities inherent in each of the languages. The English and German examples describe the complexity of the fall via a series of adverbial particles and prepositional phrases (tips him off, over a cliff, into the water, schmiß, den Abhang hinunter, ins Wasser). The verbs *tip* and *schmeißen* (hurl) signify the manner in which the deer causes the fall. The Spanish and Hebrew versions resemble each other but differ from the English and German versions. In the former pair, the event is recounted as a series of episodes. First there is a description of location (cliff with a river below, place with a swamp underneath); then the deer acts, and as a result, the boy and the dog fall. Berman and Slobin (1994, p. 12) point out that the verbs (*throw, fall, stop*) are "bare descriptions of change of state, with no elaboration of manner." Furthermore,

[t]hese are not random differences between the narrative styles of these . . . children, but rather show their abilities to convey just those analyses of the event that are most compatible with the linguistic means provided by their languages. English and German provide large sets of locative particles that can be combined with verbs of manner, thereby predisposing speakers toward a dense style of encoding motion events. On the other hand, a different style arises in other . . . languages, which rely more on simple

change of state and change of location verbs, thereby predisposing speakers towards more extended analyses of motion
events. (Berman and Slobin, 1994, p. 12)

I do not want to overemphasize the learner's first language in
the context of his or her learning a second language because
doing so runs the peril of viewing the learner's first language as a
constraining, static system from which he or she cannot escape.
It is important, however, for potential TESOLers to keep aspects
of the learner's linguistic and cultural background in mind. In
the above instance the order and manner of presentation (including addressing a problem, as well as analyzing and reasoning
through it) are conditioned in part by the linguistic resources
available and by customary modes of perception. L2 student writers, given that they have been socialized into the linguistic and
cultural practices of their respective cultures, are more likely than
native English-speaking (NES) students to encounter difficulty
when being inducted into the kind of CT practices encouraged by
writing textbooks.

Three Problematic Conduits through which
Critical Thinking Is Fostered

I took my data from 12 argument-oriented writing textbooks frequently used in L2 college-level writing classes. To ensure that
my conclusions are based on relatively recent textbooks, I used
only editions whose publication dates fall within the last 8 years
(1994 or later). The following analysis identifies conduits that all
12 texts emphasize as crucial to CT.

Conduit 1. Developing reasoning skills through informal logic
models: How general or specific a skill is CT?

Before considering whether reasoning skills can in fact be
encouraged through the teaching of informal logic, it might be
fruitful to consider whether they constitute some kind of general
ability (with general benefits) or whether they point to specific

skills (McPeck, 1990). This distinction is important because if we had some sort of mutually agreed upon idea as to the kind of competence of reasoning skills, then we would be in a better position to articulate ways of teaching that competence and testing for it. The existence of a clear, universally accepted definition would make it possible and realistic to determine what courses taught at what point in the curriculum could promote CT skills.

The writing textbooks I examined present reasoning as a general ability leading to particular benefits and as a specific skill. As I will show, this notion only complicates issues regarding whether and how reasoning skills are to be taught and tested. Reasoning skills are presented as a general ability in that they are predicated on the idea that they lead to critical thinking (Cedarblom and Paulsen, 1987; Johnson, 1992); they are presented as a specific skill in that they are seen to consist of teaching a relatively small number of specific tools that "once mastered enable one to deploy these skills across any problems, arguments, or questions where critical thinking might be called for" (McPeck, 1990, p. 24). Thus, for instance, *Writing Arguments* (Ramage and Bean, 1995) sees the function of argument as the general ability to

> think through the complexity of an issue and seek the truth. . . . The writer confident in the truth and rightness of his or her claim concentrates on swaying an audience. . . . [T]he value of referential or truth seeking argument lies in its power to deepen and complicate our understanding of the world. . . . The value of an argument with a persuasive aim is its ability to help social groups make decisions in a rational and humane way. (p. 5)

Elements of Argument (Rottenberg, 2000) adopts a similarly general stance by maintaining the importance of gauging the audience appropriately because "success is defined as acceptance of the claim by an audience. Arguers in the real world recognize intuitively that their primary goal is not to demonstrate the purity of their logic, but to win the adherence of their audiences" (p. 6).

Argumentation, for this text, has a political benefit as well. In an earlier edition of the text, Rottenberg says that "democracy depends on a citizenry that can reason for themselves, on men who know whether a case has been proved, or at least made probable" (1994, p. 7). Argumentation is seen as a "civilizing influence," "the very basis for democratic order." In free societies argument and democracy remain "the preeminent means of arriving at consensus," as opposed to totalitarian countries, where coercion may "express itself in a number of reprehensible forms—censorship, imprisonment, exile, torture, or execution" (p. 8).

All of the texts examined for this study articulate, albeit in varied ways, similar stances regarding the general benefits of critical thinking. That these texts are also simultaneously specific is partially evident in their emphasis on specific rhetorical tools, especially those oriented around "soft" logic (Scriven, 1980; Walton, 1993) as a means to target some of the general aims mentioned above. Thus, Scriven's idea that the "goal of soft logic is internalizing the skills of reasoning" (1980, p. 159) appears to be echoed in various ways in all of the examined texts. All emphasize in varying degrees aspects of informal logic considered crucial to effective and sound reasoning. *Writing Arguments* (Ramage and Bean, 1995), for instance, devotes a part of its section on Aristotelian logic to explaining the importance of assessing enthymemes in arguments. An *enthymeme* is an "incomplete logical structure that depends, for its completeness, on one or more unstated assumptions (values, beliefs, principles) that serve as the starting point of the argument" (p. 105). In their summarization of the enthymeme section, the editors lay out the following three points and an illustration supporting them:

1. Claims are supported with reasons. You can usually state a reason as a because clause attached to a claim.

2. A because clause attached to a claim is an incomplete logical structure called an enthymeme. To create a complete

logical structure from an enthymeme, the unstated assumption (or assumptions) must be articulated.

3. To serve as an effective starting point for the argument, this unstated assumption should be a belief, value, or principle that the audience grants. Let's illustrate this structure by putting the previous example—plus two new ones—into schematic form:

INITIAL ENTHYMEME: Cocaine and heroin should be legalized because legalization would eliminate the black market in drugs.

CLAIM: Cocaine and heroine should be legalized.

STATED REASON: because legalization would eliminate the black market in drugs.

UNSTATED ASSUMPTION: An action that eliminates the black market in drugs is good. (Or, to state the assumption more fully, the benefits to society of eliminating the black market in drugs outweigh the negative effects to society of legalizing drugs. (pp. 100–101)

These steps are presented as ways for the writer to arrive at unstated assumptions that an audience will (or will not) accept. This determination is important because audience acceptance at least partially influences whether the writer has grounds on which to begin building an effective argument. The successful and logical arguer, said Aristotle, is the person who knows how to formulate and develop enthymemes so that the argument hooks into the audience's values and beliefs (Ramage and Bean, 1995, p. 100).

Similar to Ramage and Bean's discussion of enthymemes in *Writing Arguments* is the section on warrants in *Elements of Argument*. Adopting the Toulmin model, *Elements of Argument* (Rottenberg, 1994) posits the importance of warrants as effective strategies by which to ensure a sound, logical relationship between a claim and support (pp. 9–11). "A warrant is an inference or an assumption . . . a guarantee of reliability" (p. 11). The following segment drawn from *Elements of Argument* (Rottenberg, 1994) stresses the importance that this text (along with the others examined) places on establishing what the given audience will consider logical connections between a claim and support:

CLAIM: Laws making marijuana illegal should be repealed.

SUPPORT: People should have the right to use any substance they wish.

WARRANT: No laws should prevent citizens from exercising their rights.

Support for repeal of the marijuana laws often consists of medical evidence that marijuana is harmless. Here, however, the author contends that an important ethical principle is at work: Nothing should prevent people from exercising their rights, including the right to use any substance, no matter how harmful. Let us suppose that the reader agrees with the supporting statement, that individuals should have the right to use any substance, no matter how harmful. But in order to accept the claim, the reader must also agree with the principle expressed in the warrant, that government should not interfere with the individual's right. He or she can then agree that laws making marijuana illegal should be repealed. *Notice that this warrant, like all warrants, certifies that the relationship between the support and the claim is sound.* (Rottenberg, 1994, p. 12, my emphasis)

Warrants, then, serve as bridges between claims and supports, as warranties that encourage skeptical audiences to be receptive to particular arguments (Ramage and Bean, 1995). In many ways they are not that different from unstated assumptions (of the kind presented earlier) in that they too are underlying beliefs that link our claims to our audience's beliefs.

One problem with these models (although they are no doubt useful in creating successful arguments) is that there appears to be much variation between textbooks as to which particular model (or set of models) actually fosters critical thinking skills. *Elements of Argument* (Rottenberg, 1994, 2000) stresses the Toulmin model (partially illustrated by the above excerpt), whereas *Writing Arguments* (Ramage and Bean, 1995) presents its discussion of enthymemes along with discussions of Aristotelian logic and the "statis system" (Fahnestock and Secor, 1991) as necessary channels through which to effect sound reasoning. Also related to the specific nature of these texts (but not particularly related to the point about informal logic) is the fact that there appears to be little agreement between these textbooks as to which specific skills inform critical thinking.

Each of the textbooks examined (to say nothing of the different programs/tests/kits/ across the country) lay differing emphases on different skills. *Writing Arguments*, for instance, partially emphasizes the *ability to detect logical fallacies*, whereas *The Informed Argument* (Miller, 1998) stresses *getting to know one's audience*. In the same vein, *Current Issues and Enduring Questions* (Barnet and Bedau, 2002) partially accentuates the difference between *reason* and *rationalization*, whereas *Contexts and Communities* (Greenberg, 1994) highlights *critical reading skills*. Arriving, thus, at a finite set of critical thinking skills about which there is mutual consensus—a feature that would facilitate its teaching and testing—when there is so much variation seems, at least for the moment, improbable. Furthermore, although the italicized phrases above are presented as specific skills that contribute to critical thinking, it could be argued that they are in fact large bundles of different kinds of skills that need to be taught and learned in more situated contexts (such as particular disciplines [Freedman, 1995; Resnick, 1990]).

Thus, the simultaneously general and specific nature of these textbooks renders them problematic. There seems to be an incongruence in the idea of exposing students to particular models of informal logic to produce an informed citizenry: the overly specific means do not exactly fit with the general ends. When such incongruent means and ends are transferred to L2 writing sections, the consequences are much more complex. Nonnative speakers of English, no matter what their technical visa status, do not necessarily come equipped with assumptions about democracy or with a general desire to be an informed citizen of the United States; as I pointed out earlier, they may also be accustomed to a different ("soft") logical system that deviates substantially from logical systems favored by U.S. institutions of learning in the frequency, distribution, and function of grammatical structures. We saw earlier that the large sets of available locative particles in English and German may partially account for the increased use of location descriptors by native speakers of these languages; spoken discourse in Spanish and Hebrew, on the other hand, does not offer as many locative particles (Berman and Slobin, 1994). L2 student writers, then, expected to structure their information in ways that meet the discourse expectations of their English-speaking audiences (Ramanathan-Abbott, 1993), are doubly disadvantaged: they are not likely to have been socialized into North American middle-class literacy practices that would facilitate mastery over these models, and they are more likely to have been socialized into other linguistic systems that employ different logics to address problems and the structuring of information.

Conduit 2. Encouraging reasoning/critical thinking skills by developing and refining students' problem-solving skills

Critical thinking experts such as Ennis (1987) and Johnson (1992) want to collapse notions of reasoning ability and everyday problems to argument analysis. "More often than not, they go on to collapse these distinctions by simply talking about 'everyday reasoning'—a phrase which has a nice ring about it, if for no other reason than it suggests something which is clear and understood by everybody" (McPeck, 1990, p. 1). Scriven (1992) maintains that training in critical thinking should include highly controversial issues of considerable personal, social, or intellectual importance that are not seriously addressed in the regular curriculum. Arguments, as presented in the examined texts, appear to reflect this view: the subject matter for most of them subsumes everyday matters of public controversy or social problems that concentrate on current sociopolitical issues such as nuclear armament, the right to die, gays in the military, gun control, animal experimentation, illegal immigration, affirmative action, and women's rights, to name a few. Reflection on and exploration of such everyday arguments is regarded as healthy and desirable because the "argumentative process . . . is indispensable to the preservation of a free society" (Rottenberg, 1994, p. 5). Such a view is justified on at least the following points: (1) the survival of a democracy depends partially on public debate about such issues, (2) public education in North America would like to prepare people to make decisions about such issues, and (3) these are areas around which honest disagreement is possible (McPeck, 1990).

The following cases, taken from the introductory chapter of *Writing Arguments* (Ramage and Bean, 1995), illustrate the sociopolitical nature of some of these problems:

CASE ONE
ILLINOIS COURT WON'T HEAR CASE OF MOM WHO REFUSES SURGERY
CHICAGO—A complex legal battle over a Chicago woman's refusal to undergo a cesarean section, even though it could save the life of her unborn child, essentially was settled yesterday when the state's highest court refused to hear the case.

The court declined to review a lower court's ruling that the woman should not be forced to submit to surgery in a case that pitted the rights of the woman, referred to in court as "Mother Doe," against those of her fetus.

The 22-year-old Chicago woman, now in her 37th week of pregnancy, refused her doctor's advice to have the surgery because she believes God intended her to deliver the child naturally.

The woman's attorneys argued that the operation would violate her constitutional rights and the free operation of her religious beliefs.

Cook County Public Guardian Patrick Murphy, the court-appointed representative of the woman's fetus, said he would petition with the Supreme Court asking it to hear the case. He has 90 days to file the petition, but he acknowledged future action would probably come too late.

Doctors say the fetus is not receiving enough oxygen from the placenta and will either die or be retarded unless it is delivered by cesarean section. Despite that diagnosis, the mother has stressed her faith in God's healing powers and refused [her] doctor's advice to submit to the operation. (pp. 11–12)

CASE TWO
HOMELESS HIT THE STREETS TO PROTEST BAN
SEATTLE—The homeless stood up for themselves by sitting down in a peaceful but vocal protest yesterday in Seattle's University District.

About 50 people met at noon to criticize a proposed set of city ordinances that would ban panhandlers from sitting on sidewalks, put them in jail for repeatedly urinating in public, and crack down on "intimidating" street behavior.

"Sitting is not a crime," read poster boards that feature mug shots of Seattle City Attorney Mark Sidran, who is pushing for the new laws. . . . "This is city property; the police want to tell us that we can't sit here," yelled one man named R. C. as he sat cross-legged outside a pizza establishment.

Marsha Shaiman stood outside the University Book Store holding a poster and waving it at passing cars. She is not homeless, but was one of many activists in the crowd. "I qualify as a privileged white yuppie," she said. "I am offended that the privileged people in this country are pointing at the poor, and people of color, and say they are causing problems. They are being used as scapegoats."

Many local merchants support the ban, saying that panhandlers hurt business by intimidating shoppers and fouling the area with the odor of urine, vomited wine, and sometimes even feces. (p. 13)

Presenting cases/problems such as these is intended to induce students "to see argument first as a process of truth-seeking and clarification and then later, when you are firmly committed to a position, as an occasion for persuasion" (Ramage and Bean, 1995, p. 22). The textbook advises students to seek out a wide range of views, to welcome views different from their own, to treat these views respectfully, and to see them as intelligent and rationally defensible. The skills of reason and inquiry developed through the writing of arguments is meant to help students become more objective by enabling them to present sound arguments.

These laudable goals pose at least two problems. In all of the examined texts, social problems are presented with pro and con readings that are intended to provide students with different viewpoints so as to enable them to take an informed stand. However, having students take a stand and make sound judgments after having read three or four pro and con readings on such complicated issues as affirmative action or euthanasia does not prepare them to deal with the issue in its complexities at all; if anything, this practice takes away from the enormous complexities built into these issues, turning real problems into pseudoproblems with easy solutions.

A second problem with this conduit has to do with the fact that informal logic tools of the kind discussed earlier are used to perform sound analyses on such everyday social problems. Like McPeck (1990), I contend that the real difficulty with everyday social problems has little to do with establishing soundness and almost everything to do with understanding and assimilating complex information. You can pick virtually any everyday problem and find yourself sinking into a quagmire of arguments and counterarguments. For example, the issue of gays in the military opens up, among others, questions about religious/moral attitudes toward homosexuality, about judging military ability on the basis of sexual preference, about being public or not about sexual identity, about equal rights, and even about the possibility of women serving in the military. Making a truly sound decision about these kinds of issues would mean having access to a lot of information.

In the end, whatever stand we take is tenuous because there are few simple and straightforward decisions in these matters—a point that is conceded by at least five of the examined texts. It follows that students need much more than three or four readings to make any kind of informed judgment. As for L2 student writers, given that they have not necessarily been socialized in this culture, they may not perceive alleged problems as problems at all, or even as matters of particular interest. As Kaplan and I argue elsewhere (Ramanathan and Kaplan, 1996a), a topic such as gun control may not be seen as a problem by individuals from cultures in which guns are prohibited entirely, and individuals from other cultures may not understand the implied constitutional right to bear arms that, among other issues, underlies the gun-control debate in the United States.

Conduit 3. Developing the ability to look for hidden assumptions and fallacies in everyday arguments.

This point integrates parts of conduit 1 (the use of informal logic tools) and conduit 2 (namely everyday arguments) to address the importance of looking for logical fallacies and hidden assumptions. All of the textbooks stress the ability to discern logical flaws in one's own and others' argumentation process as crucial to the development of critical reading/writing skills. *The Informed Argument* (Miller, 1998), for instance, lists 14 common fallacies of which the *ad hominem* argument, *ad misericordiam* argument, *ad populum* argument, slippery slope, and straw man are a few (pp. 29–35). The following steps illustrate the text's explanation of two of these terms:

Sliding Down a Slippery Slope

According to this fallacy, one step will inevitably lead to an undesirable second step. An example would be claiming that legalized abortion will lead to euthanasia or that censoring pornography will lead to the end of the freedom of the press. Although it is important to consider the probable effects of any step that is being debated, it is fallacious to claim that men and women will necessarily tumble downhill as a result of any one step. There is always the possibility that we'll be able to keep our feet firmly on the ground even though we've moved them from where they used to be. (pp. 45–46)

Opposing a Straw Man

Because it is easier to demolish a man of straw than to address a live opponent fairly, arguers are sometimes tempted to pretend that they are responding to the views of their opponents when they are only setting up a type of artificial opposition which they can easily refute. The most common form of this fallacy is to exaggerate the views of others or to respond only to an extreme view that does not adequately represent the arguments of one's opponents. If you argue against abolishing Social Security, you should not think that you have defended that program from all its critics. By responding only to an extreme position, you would be doing nothing to resolve specific concerns about how Social Security is financed and administered. (p. 44)

The Informed Argument partially justifies its list of various kinds of fallacies on the grounds that some writers and speakers deliberately use them for winning an argument and that it is important to be alert for these in others' arguments. Fine. But what purpose does a list or an exercise in fallacy hunting serve in creating sound arguments? Even if students learn to discover fallacies in an argument, they are still not going to be able to infer that the opposing side has won or is preferable. At best all that can be inferred is that this specific argument is fallacious. It is still not enough basis on which to be able to take a stand on an everyday argument.

The suggested activity of seeking unstated assumptions is equally problematic in the textbooks. *CIEQ*, (1993) for example, provides the following example of unstated assumptions in an argument on abortion:

1. Ours is a pluralistic society, in which we believe that religious beliefs of one group should not be imposed on others.
2. Personal privacy is a right, and [a] woman's body is hers, not to be violated by laws that tell her she cannot do certain things to her body. But these and other arguments assume that a fetus is not—or not yet—a person, and therefore is not entitled to protection against assaults. Virtually all of us assume that it is wrong to kill a human being. Granted, we may find instances in which we believe it acceptable to take a human life, such as self-defense against a would-be-murderer, but everywhere we find a shared assumption that persons are ordinarily entitled to not be killed.

The argument about abortion, then, usually depends on opposed assumptions. For one group, the fetus is a human being and a potential person—and this potentiality is decisive. But for the other group it is not. Persons arguing one side or the other of the abortion issue ought to be aware that opponents may not share their assumptions. (p. 35)

On the face of it, the preceding example seems straightforward enough. Although *CIEQ*'s assumptions about a fetus not being entitled to protection against assaults and of all living persons being entitled to life are viable assumptions, they constitute only one set of assumptions. As McPeck (1990) contends, there is no method of determining what other assumptions the author might be making partly because there is a potentially indeterminate number of assumptions underlying any given premise, and each of these possible assumptions may have an indeterminate number of assumptions underlying it. The different kinds of assumptions that we have seen from Walton (1993) for avoiding a "straw man" and "making minimal assumptions" seem designed to create new assumptions about the argument rather than uncovering unexamined beliefs or hidden assumptions. The analyst—in the present case the L1 and L2 student writer—seems to be engaged in such a process; students learn to infer assumptions even though those assumptions may not necessarily be implied by the argument. As McPeck warns us, this can be "very dangerous business, indeed, not only because it can easily strap someone with an assumption that they were not in fact making but also because it threatens to strip argument analysis of its objective integrity by encouraging subjective interpretations" (1990, p. 8).

Moving Critical Thinking into the Bigger Picture: Generalizing the Discussion

An assumption in the CT practice—and one that has been lurking beneath this discussion—concerns the relatively unproblematic way in which critical thinking skills are generally seen to be useful and transferable across knowledge domains (Glaser, 1984). Knowledge transfer, as research shows us, is a debated notion: On the one hand, researchers such as Rubenstein and Firstenberg (1987) maintain that higher-order abilities such as problem solving and deductive competence can be taught through informal logic tools that will enable learners to reason successfully. This group of scholars, who believe that domain-specific knowledge is not conducive to "good thinking" (Nickerson 1987), cite research in cognitive science, developmental psychology, and human intelligence to support their stand. In fact, Glaser believes that

[a] student does not tend "naturally" to develop a general dis-

position to consider thoughtfully the subjects and problems that come within the range of his or her experience; nor is he or she likely to acquire knowledge of the methods of logical inquiry and reasoning and skill in applying these methods simply as a result of having studied this subject or that. There is little evidence that students acquire skill in critical thinking as a necessary by-product of the study of [any] given language. (1984, p. 27)

Scholars such as Butterfield and Nelson (1991) and McPeck (1990), however, lean toward the other side in their skepticism about a general system of logical competence. They prefer to see thought processes as situated and highly content and context dependent. Evans (1982), in fact, is

forced to the conclusion that people manifest little ability for general deductive reasoning in these experiments. Very little behavior can be attributed to an a priori system that is independent of the particular task content and structure. This does not mean that people cannot reason correctly in contexts where they have no relevant and appropriate experience—indeed some evidence suggests that they can. It does mean, however, that adults' reasoning ability is far more concrete and context-dependent than has been generally believed. (p. 254)

Butterfield and Nelson's views (1991) also problematize the idea that reasoning skills can cut across knowledge domains. According to them, the general consensus on the transfer of instruction is that "the majority of investigations have not found flexible use of appropriate variants of taught knowledge and strategies in diverse contexts and for diverse purposes" (p. 69).

Although some level of transferability might be possible across some knowledge domains—whether at a macro level of critical thinking (Greenfield, 1987) or at a micro level of specific information processing—the point I want to underscore is that the transfer and general applicability of critical thinking/reasoning skills is at best a debatable one. Thus, for so many writing textbooks—indeed writing programs, syllabi, and other pedagogical tools—to be based on such grounds is cause for serious reconsideration.

Audience and Voice in Writing Textbooks

I turn now to *audience* and *voice*—notions that to some extent overlap with and are embedded in *critical thinking* (given that writers who evidence critical thinking in their writing are generally considered capable of manipulating their voice to suit their audience). L2 teachers of writing at a variety of levels may tell their students, "Consider what you think your audience needs to know" and "I don't hear you in this essay; you need to develop and present your voice more strongly." Such comments assume that students know for whom they are writing and that they should be able to articulate ideas tailored to the needs of this audience (Park, 1982, 1986). Also implicit is the idea that presenting a strong, individualized self in writing is not problematic (Ramanathan and Atkinson, 1999; Scollon, 1991; Scollon and Scollon, 1981) and that asserting and supporting one's position(s) in writing is simply "how it is done." All TESOLers need to examine, question, and possibly change such "commonsensical" givens.

The view of the writer as able to present a strong voice only when he or she has a clear sense of audience is based on the premise accepted by most researchers who believe that all writing is context based and socially constructed (e.g., Bazerman, 1988; Bizzell, 1992; Brandt, 1986; Swales, 1990). Such a view is central to writing instruction in composition programs in North America, and current curricula, textbooks, pedagogy, and syllabi typically stress the importance of developing student voices by sensitizing student writers to the expectations of their audience (Atkinson and Ramanathan, 1995; Mangelsdorf, Roen, and Taylor, 1990). It is important for L2 teachers to recognize that notions of audience and voice are difficult even for mainstream students, which is evident in the problems they encounter in the writing process and in the numerous comments teachers make on their essays regarding these notions. They are even more problematic for students from non-U.S. cultures (Mangelsdorf et al., 1990). Part of the difficulty with notions of audience and voice arises from the fact that these terms point to concepts that are largely culturally constrained and relatively inaccessible to students who are not full participants in the culture within which they are asked to write. The problem may also stem from an inductive approach to teaching writing that encourages students to discover form in the process of writing (e.g., Freedman, 1995; Harris, 1990). The following sections address these points.

Writing, the Inductive Approach, and Non-U.S. Student Writers

Before discussing some underlying assumptions in current tertiary-level writing textbooks, I want to clarify what I mean by the inductive approach and problems inherent in it. One of several approaches to teaching writing, the phrase *inductive approach* refers specifically to pedagogical practices that eschew the explicit teaching of written forms in favor of encouraging students to discover form in their writing process. According to Coe (1987), proponents of this approach believe that "form grows organically to fit the shape of the subject matter," that there is "little need to teach form except as an afterthought (along with punctuation) late in both the teaching and writing processes" (p. 16). This organic growth of form and structure in the writing process is seen to transform the writer's "interior text" (Harris, 1990), which is often fragmentary and located in the mind of the writer, into a text that is more pragmatic and that reflects the writer's awareness of the rhetorical situation and the reader/audience. This transformation is seen to occur as a natural part of the writing process. It is important to note, however, that contradictions exist between an emphasis on implemented pedagogical approaches and expectation of written product. As Inghileri (1989) points out, "Teachers introduce activities associated with process writing while orienting students toward a particular form. This form is not made explicit so as to develop their writing without the pressure of the product in mind" (p. 392). Students—especially nonnative students—are particularly vulnerable to the negative ramifications of this equation. Not only do they have to discover what they want to say, but they have to say it in a form that meets the discourse expectations of the teacher/reader (Ramanathan-Abbott, 1993).

Like Harris (1990) and other process-oriented researchers, Freedman (1995) believes that form arises from content and need not be explicitly taught. On the basis of her observations of undergraduate law students, Freedman maintains that these students acquired writing skills that were expected of law students *without* being explicitly taught genre rules. However, as much content-based writing literature suggests (e.g., Gilbert and Mulkay, 1984; Swales, 1987), a learner can be apprenticed to a master craftsperson to learn how to use a disciplinary text. That law students seem to acquire a legal writing style derives not from some inexplicit process but from the fact that they read legal texts, have a high degree of motivation to enter the legal discourse community, and have access to their teachers' repeated modeling for legal texts; in other words, they are steeped in the social practices of their TCs.

Likewise, recent ethnographic research on cultural differences in approaches to teaching writing in an ESL institute and a composition program at a large U.S. university (Atkinson and Ramanathan, 1995) points to ways in which teaching strategies and socialization practices in the university's composition program favor an inductive (implicit) approach over a deductive (explicit) one. Because the student population in the composition program consists predominantly of mainstream U.S. students (less than 20 percent are nonnative speakers [NNS]), teaching strategies adopted in the composition program tend to assume a set of cultural norms that many ESL students encounter in their transition from L2 to L1 programs. As I mentioned earlier, L1 students have a relatively easier time in writing classes because of their early socialization into essayist literacy (e.g., Gee, 1990; Heath, 1983; Scollon and Scollon, 1981), which begins in early childhood in middle-class homes, is reinforced through elementary and high school years, and is assumed of literate middle-class adults in higher education and beyond. Thus, teachers customarily perceived as teaching writing skills may in fact be providing mainstream students with opportunities to enhance and refine competencies that the students have been acquiring all their lives.

An inductive, inexplicit approach to the teaching of composition, then, embraces problems of varying natures and complexities. Yet as problematic as this approach is, it continues to influence composition programs across the United States; indeed, several writing textbooks—along with course descriptions, syllabi, and pedagogical tools—clearly favor this approach. *Current Issues and Enduring Questions* contains the following excerpt on audience. It should be noted, however, that equally problematic instructions on how to imagine an audience can be taken from virtually any composition text:

> Of course the questions that you ask yourself . . . [in imagining your audience] will depend on what you are writing about, but five additional questions are always relevant:
>
> 1. Who are my readers?
> 2. What do they believe?
> 3. How much common ground do we share?
> 4. What do I want my readers to believe?
> 5. What do they need to know?
>
> These questions require little comment. The literal answer to the first is probably "the teacher," but (unless you are given instructions to the contrary) you should not write specifically for the teacher; instead you should write for an audience that is, generally speaking, like your classmates. In short, your imagined audience is literate, intelligent, and moderately well-informed, but it does not know everything that you know, and it does not know your response to the problem you are addressing. (Barnet and Bedau, 1999, p. 167)

This kind of guidance is ineffective for any number of reasons. Most notably, it is unrealistic. In most situations—and in virtually every situation in composition classes—students realize that they are writing for an audience much more critically oriented than their classmates. Also, assuming that the instructor has personally chosen the material for his or her class, *CIEQ*'s suggestion that the imagined audience "does not know everything you know" is simply not viable. An intimidating and often frustrating reality for students is that their instructor will usually know everything they know, and more, about the subject in question.

This is not to say that *CIEQ* is a poor writing text; on the contrary, it offers an impressive array of substantive readings and valuable guidelines for creating successful arguments. The inductive approach that it adopts toward the teaching of audience and voice, however, is disturbingly simplistic and typical of many texts, and presenting a list of "always relevant questions" (a practice recommended in several L2 and L1 writing books) is not the most effective way of sensitizing student writers—native speaking, but especially nonnative speaking—to these concepts. Potential L2 teachers need to be aware that the presentation of the terms *audience* and *voice* in many writing textbooks excludes learners whose first language is not English from engaging in a potential dialogue with the textbooks, thus inhibiting students' development as full participants in any academic discourse community.

Audience and Voice in Composition/Writing Texts

I examine some problems inherent in notions of audience and voice as these concepts are presented in tertiary-level instructional texts.[1] In the practices that follow, the capital A or V before each of these points/assumptions signifies whether the point addresses audience or voice. These letters do not by any means indicate hard and fast connections to their respective points, only relative ones. There is much overlap between audience and voice regarding these points because so much of voice depends on audience and vice versa. All of the points are predicated on a relatively high degree of shared cultural knowledge, and all of them are issues that L2 teachers need to be aware of, especially when considering adopting texts for their classes. The following is a partial list of mainstream college-level writing practices in this culture that are often problematic for nonnative students.

> Point 1 (V). That the essay makes a point: it has a focus and other points are subordinated to this larger focus.

This idea is problematic for several reasons. First, most L1 and L2 writing textbooks assume that the linear, thesis-driven model of writing is a universal rhetorical structure, and second, that such a rhetorical structure is most conducive to the development and presentation of a strong, individualized voice. Not only has much research in contrastive rhetoric pointed out that rhetorical structures across cultures vary, but the idea that a person must present a strong voice in writing is not necessarily favored by other cultures. ESL student writers, then, often find themselves locked out of the reader-writer transaction: not only do they frequently come to the writing task having been socialized into structuring texts in different ways, but they are often unfamiliar with the notion of presenting strong, individualized voices or the need for such an approach (Ramanathan and Atkinson, 1999). Making TESOLers conscious of the possible cultural dissonance between the teaching materials (textbooks, course curricula, course descriptions) they adopt and the cultural and educational backgrounds of their ESL students will allow them to contextualize their teaching in ways that mitigate the gulf.

> Point 2 (A). That a strong essay concerns an arguable issue: a strong argument deals with an issue that divides an audience.

Being able to assess what constitutes an arguable issue assumes a sense of audience for whom a particular issue is arguable, and a majority of writing assignments that composition programs encourage are predicated on such audience awareness.

Assignments on abortion, euthanasia, animal rights, or gun control are embedded in social issues privileged by this culture. They assume an awareness of audiences that will be divided on these issues; they also assume an awareness of political and/or ethical stances that mark these different audiences. Such presuppositions pose problems for students who do not share "appropriate" cultural frames. Enrolled TESOLers need to be aware of the importance of gradually expanding the sociocognitive maps of their ESL students if they design and use assignments around these issues.

Point 3 (A). That a strong argument makes intertextual connections: a strong argument's persuasive quality derives from the way writers borrow and stitch together bits of old texts to create a new text.

Being able to make intertextual references in a person's new text demonstrates an awareness of prior/old texts. Porter (1986) makes a distinction between two kinds of intertextuality: iterability and presupposition. "Iterability refers to the repeatability of certain textual fragments, to citations within a discourse, but also unannounced sources and influences, clichés, phrases in the air, and traditions" (p. 35). Thus, every text relies partially on other texts for its meaning. Presupposition, in contrast, refers to assumptions a text makes about its referent, its readers, and its context—"to portions of the text which are read, but which are not explicitly 'there'" (p. 35). "Once upon a time" is, according to Porter, a rhetorical presupposition: it signals even to the youngest mainstream reader the opening of a mythic story. New texts, then, appropriate other texts through both implicit and explicit reference. Depending on the degree of shared cultural knowledge that ESL student writers possess, they may or may not recognize such intertextual maneuverings, let alone successfully integrate them into their own writings. Although they may be able to draw on old texts from their respective cultures, these texts are often rendered irrelevant because of the nature of topics assigned in mainstream writing/composition programs. Making potential L2 teachers aware of the numerous assumptions latent in writing assignments they give their ESL students and enabling them to uncover some of these assumptions for themselves is a first step in making them critical language teachers.

Point 4 (V). That a strong argument uses reason: a strong argument displays evidence of critical thought.

Many writing texts are oriented toward developing student voices through the teaching of reasoning skills, which are assumed to be culture-free and to operate on the basis of a universal logic. As with points 2 and 3, being able to think critically—at least as presented in these textbooks—is predicated on the assumption that the student is acculturated enough to see relationships among various cultural phenomena (e.g., that increasing crime in U.S. inner cities could be, in part, a result of easy availability of guns), to assess the credibility of different kinds of sources (e.g., that citing from a well-established academic journal may be more credible than citing from *Newsweek* or *Time*), and to weigh various kinds of evidence (e.g., evidence gathered on the basis of a well-conducted study is probably more credible that evidence presented on a TV talk show). The cultural mainstream in the United States places high value on all of these skills, but such is not necessarily the case in other cultures.

Point 5 (A). That the writer is aware of the topic's complexity: a sound argument recognizes that there are no simple solutions to social issues; most issues involve various complexities.

Mainstream U.S. culture recognizes, for instance, that gun control is a complex issue and that any attempt to address it must deal with uncovering and acknowledging the intricacies involved. This would mean identifying *what* the audience cares about (or does not care about) and identifying *why* it maintains the stand it does. It is the writer's responsibility to present relevant information regarding the topic in question in order to communicate effectively—a feature that may not be necessarily shared by all cultures. Hinds (1987) and Yoshikawa (1978) suggest that some cultures lay greater emphasis on the participation of the *reader/listener* for effective communication—that is, it is the audience's responsibility to intuit and understand the complexities inherent in what their writer or speaker says or intends to say.

Point 6 (V). That a strong argument incorporates values: the act of writing/reasoning forces individuals to rethink their values and beliefs.

Many writing textbooks stress the idea that the act of writing facilitates reevaluation of an individual's values and beliefs and that this process is a necessary component of developing a person's voice. These texts assume that rethinking old views about issues through intelligent questions is a positive and crucial process in developing writing skills. Socialized in largely Socratic methods of teaching (Scollon, 1999), mainstream ESL teachers need to recognize the cultural presuppositions of their modes of teaching and ways in which their teaching preferences do or do not cause cultural dissonance for their students, thereby hindering effective teaching and learning.

Point 7 (A). That a strong argument has an audience: a sound argument will consider its audience's needs.

This point assumes the consideration of basic questions: How informed is my audience? How much knowledge do we share? Which terms and concepts need defining? What can I assume my audience will know? Current writing/composition textbooks emphasize the need to establish common ground with those prepared to disagree with the individual's stand, the assumption being that "we can present our views most effectively if we acknowledge those ideas and values that we share with opponents" (Seyler, 1991, p. 72). The value that mainstream U.S. society places on explicit, decontextualized information that is relatively decodable in other contexts by other people in both speaking and writing, but especially in writing (Gee, 1990; Ramanathan-Abbott, 1993), is not necessarily shared by its own African-American culture or some Asian cultures (Eggington, 1987; Hinds, 1987). Because audience participation in both the text's construction and interpretation may be greater in these cultures, the need for being explicit in writing may not be seen as necessary.

> Point 8 (V). That a strong argument recognizes counter-positions: an effective argument recognizes alternative viewpoints.

Central to effective writing in this culture is the author's ability to present a reasoned and balanced consideration of other points of view while promoting his or her own (Ferris, 1994). Being able to position and advance your voice along with other countervoices is seen as a persuasive strategy that strengthens the rationality of your stand. The effectiveness of your argument is judged partly in terms of the cerebral (rational) quality of its appeal, drawn in part from this dialogue between your own voice and other counter-voices. Arguments in other cultures, especially those with strong oral traditions, may not derive their persuasive power primarily through rational, reasoned appeals but from emotional ones. Once again, it is important for potential L2 teachers to be aware of the cultural leanings in their expectations of how and in what ways students advance their opinions in writing.

Audience, Voice, and Critical Thinking: Implications for TESOLers

Having examined some ways that particular problematic features of teaching materials can be taken apart and analyzed carefully, we need to ask what a solution to these problems might be. Although any solution we come up with may be an idealized one—given that most solutions regarding such matters are going to require serious revamping of curricular materials, programs, syllabi, textbooks—it is crucial that we push toward articulating solutions because they are the necessary first steps to effect any kind of change, whether it be in the individual classroom or in the discipline. Thus, one solution for the problems inherent in notions of audience, voice, and critical thinking might be contextualizing them within specific disciplinary communities.

The kind of voice and critical thinking that writing textbooks encourage students to develop is decontextualized in at least two ways. First, these terms are not anchored in specific genres except in the "supergenre" of the academic essay, a form that students are not likely to use outside the writing classroom. And second, neither voice nor critical thinking addresses any specific disciplinary community/TC. The "always relevant questions" cited in *CIEQ*—Who are my readers? What do they believe? How much common ground do we share? What do I want my readers to believe? What do they need to know?—are, in this regard, not only amorphous but unanswerable because they are not tailored to particular genres or specifiable audiences. The same holds for the idea that we can look for "hidden assumptions in everyday arguments" by developing problem-solving skills and using informal logic tools. These skills are hard to develop outside of rules, requirements, or constraints of particular disciplines.

On the other hand, discipline-oriented writing, especially in advanced writing courses, might mitigate some of the problems implicit in these notions. Each discipline/TC constitutes its own culture in the sense that each has its own conventions and rules regarding what characterizes effective and appropriate writing for that discipline. Each uses and writes the English language differently—for different purposes, about different things, in different formats. Each is its own thought collective. As I pointed out in chapters 1 and 2, students, researchers, mentors, faculty members—in short, all who participate in the discipline and have their professional cognitions shaped by it—constitute that discipline's TC. To be considered a full and participating member of the community,

> a speaker must be "qualified" to talk; he has to belong to a community of scholarship; and he is required to possess a prescribed body of knowledge (doctrine). . . . [This system] operates to constrain discourse; it establishes limits and regularities. . . . When applied to discourse, the various rules and practices of exclusion, in fact, designate systematically

who may speak, what may be spoken, and how it is to be
said; in addition, they prescribe what is true and what is
false, what is reasonable and what is foolish, and what is
meant and what is not. (Leitch, 1983, p. 145)

Each of the eight points in this chapter can be addressed from
this standpoint. Consider, for example, the first point, regarding
the effective presentation of voice through the establishment of a
central point. Different TCs place different emphases on the role
of the author's voice in the presentation of information and on
the author's stance with respect to text and the audience (Kaplan
et al., 1994). The sciences and the social sciences, for instance,
typically discourage the use of personal pronouns, active-voice
verbs, and stylish prose, whereas the humanities often encourage
them (Bazerman, 1988).

Also, as I pointed out in chapter 3, various TCs present information differently because they use genres and writing conventions differently: a publishable manuscript in the social sciences,
for instance, often includes certain sectioning conventions, such
as a review of prior research, methods, results, and discussion.
On a more essential level, a manuscript must reveal certain characteristics and have an *ethos* (in the broadest sense) conforming
to the standards of the TC: "It must demonstrate (or at least
claim) that it contributes knowledge to the field, [and] it must
demonstrate familiarity with the work of previous researchers in
the field" (Porter, 1986, pp. 39–40). Thus, a text is acceptable
within a community (TC) only insofar as it adheres to that community's worldview. A discipline-oriented approach to writing
would mean that the student—especially the L2 student—would
gain awareness of the kind of writing most effective in his or her
chosen discipline. This might reduce the problems faced by nonnative English-speaking students who must write in an unfamiliar essay genre for a vaguely defined general audience.

Having the content of the discipline dictate writing assignments might also reduce problems inherent in points 2, 3, 4, 5,
and 8. Discerning what constitutes an arguable issue (#2), mak-

ing intertextual connections between disparate elements (#3), recognizing a topic's complexity (#4), demonstrating sound reasoning (#5), and recognizing counterpositions (#8) will possibly become clearer in a disciplinary context. Locating assignments within their discipline will familiarize students not only with real and complex issues but also with crucial old and new texts, as well as with counterpositions and reasoning strategies in the discipline. It follows, too, that such awareness could generate a clearer sense of what constitutes relevant evidence. English-speaking students—both native and nonnative—can gather appropriate evidence and support only after they have a sense of how much their writing topic is an issue. An awareness of both issues and relevant evidence will influence the kind of reasoning—and, by extension, voice—they use in their writing—a point already addressed by much research in L1 writing. Some current writing texts and assignments, on the other hand, assume that values can be rethought by raising critical intelligent questions (#6), an assumption predicated on the fallacy that critical intelligent questions are culture- or discipline-free.

If one of our aims as effective L2 teachers is to enhance the communicative competence of our nonnative English-speaking college students by enabling them to write critically by developing voices in relation to their audiences, then it is crucial that we provide them with a viable context—in this case a discipline—with which to do so. It is also crucial that all ESL people—especially educators and L2 teachers—engage in becoming meta-aware of what we bring to the L2 classroom and of the latent sociocultural politics of the texts and teaching practices we employ. It is imperative for us to engage in complex text analysis because, as this chapter's epigraph reminds us, "texts do not always mean or communicate what they say." It seems to be no small matter that so many writing textbooks fail to observe what they profess: a consideration of their nonmainstream audiences.

Chapter 5

Politics, Again: Some Practical Ways to Build Meta-Awareness into (L1 and) L2 Teacher Education

Knowledges, as with any cultural artifact, do more than they purport to do. Many of the contributions to contemporary cultural studies have occupied themselves with this "more," arguing that science, law, and theology, for example, function as "discursive formations," as much as in the business of ruling and marginalizing peoples as they dispense the knowledges they own up to. While this perspective is one we cannot shrink from, contemporary studies of culture have left us a legacy more unsettling in its main features. For the "more" that knowledges do and say is not principally a kind of lie; nor is it an impurity [of which] we can rid ourselves. . . . On the contrary, those of us who engage in knowledge production . . . are, in fact, producers of culture. . . . Today in the classroom, I can no longer limit myself to the instruction of my students into the ideas and methods of social science. The practice of [the TC] also requires the cultivation of a trait of twentieth-century culture . . . of being in culture while scrutinizing it.

—E. Doyle McCarthy, *Knowledge as Culture*

The kind of self-reflexive turn that this epigraph and that much of this book insists on hinges on an awareness of two central aspects of TCs discussed in chapter 1: (1) that knowledges and cultures of TCs shape and ultimately produce particular kinds of participants, text types, and social practices and (2) that we as participants, in turn, by engaging in certain social practices and by reproducing particular (dominant) alignments, shape and ultimately produce our TCs. Indeed, all of the intervening chapters have been devoted to uncovering aspects of how knowledges and cultures in (TESOL) TCs are produced, sustained, and reproduced and how interpretations of these processes are selective. Toward amalgamating key implications of the earlier chapters into relatively practical suggestions for enhancing (L2) teacher education, I begin the discussion in this chapter by first summarizing some key points already covered in order to better address the notion of alignment that has thus far remained latent in the general discussion.

Devoted to addressing issues in the smaller TC of individual programs, the findings in chapter 3 raise questions regarding what the divergence between two MA-TESOL programs means for the larger field of TESOL. We saw that the program at WCU, part of a linguistics department, has a strong structural/general linguistics slant built into its curriculum, whereas the program at SEU, part of an English department, lays particular emphasis on writing/composition—crucial differences that, among other factors, shape how each program trains its potential L2 teachers. Each program sustains its culture because of particular alignments among the various components and constraints that make it up, including curriculum demands, local budgets, campuswide demands, community needs, disciplinary orientations, and types of students. Addressing some of the local ways that the two smaller TCs differ from each other facilitates meta-awareness relevant to the larger TC, namely what this divergence means for the discipline and whether TESOL should think about coming up with criteria for tertiary-level ESL education.

Moving beyond the realm of small TCs, chapter 4 addresses issues related to genres and text types. Also assuming a self-reflective stance, this chapter discusses ways in which particular social practices in both applied linguistics/TESOL and other disciplines keep certain genres stable, whereas other practices lead to genre changes. As with chapter 3, the larger point of this chapter is to heighten awareness of how all of us in TESOL/applied linguistics contribute to the stability or evolution of textual forms by participating in the very social practices in which particular text types are embedded. Chapter 5, becoming more specific, is oriented to addressing a particular set of pedagogical tools, namely writing textbooks, and the importance of encouraging potential (L2) teachers to uncover some cultural assumptions in the tools they adopt, while being mindful of not letting culture become a static, all-encompassing category.

Each of the disciplinary components I have examined—individual programs, genres, textbooks—exerts a kind of authority that legitimates particular versions of "commonsensical" attitudes regarding the way things are in the discipline/s. What is at issue here is not simply how particular disciplinary facets function to reference forms of sociopolitical and sociocognitive relations but how "power works both as a medium and as an outcome" (Aronowitz and Giroux, 1993) of what might be called the "politics of official knowledge" in TCs. As we have seen in the previous chapters, official knowledge operates as a medium for socializing potential TESOLers and as an outcome by producing cohorts of trained teachers. We also saw its simultaneously pedagogical and sociopolitical nature. It is sociopolitical in that it offers participants certain subject positions and ideological references that influence the professional cognitions of TESOLers. As part of pedagogical practice, official knowledge has to be addressed not simply as reflective of the TC's ideology but as "part of a wider circuit of power that calls into play broader institutional practices and social structures" (Aronowitz and Giroux, 1993, p. 215). Given all of its dimensions, official knowledge should be viewed not as something that "comes down to us" but as a multifaceted, contested site that invites critical examination and, where relevant, change.

Implicit in the analysis and discussion of the previous chapters is the idea that specific facets of TCs align (Wartenberg, 1990) with each other in certain ways to produce particular pockets of knowledges and perspectives:

A field of social agents can constitute an alignment in regard to a social agent if and only if, first of all, their actions in regard to that agent are coordinated in a specific manner. To be in alignment, however, the coordinated practices of these social agents need to be comprehensive enough that the social agent facing the alignment encounters that alignment as having control over certain things that she might either need or desire. . . . The concept of a social alignment pro- vides a way of understanding the "field" that constitutes a situated power relationship as a power relationship. (War- tenberg, 1990; cited by Rouse, 1994)

Viewing the emergence, development, sustenance, and repro- duction of cognitions of all TESOLers as being distributed across and aligned with genres, texts, books, research agendas, propos- als, conferences, mentoring, and publishing allows us to see how positions of relative power get assigned, circulated, and rein- forced through the collective, with groups of scholars promoting certain stances on particular debates, which may (or may not, depending on the thought styles developed by other groups of scholars) render their work as being the current, privileged set of hot topics and debates of the TCs. Indeed, recent debates regard- ing the political versus pragmatic aspects of language teaching or critical thinking in undergraduate writing textbooks or the trans- ferability of Western-style teaching practices in non-Western cul- tural contexts are some examples of controversies that have drawn sets of researchers to align themselves with certain research camps.

This kind of building up and spreading of particular knowl- edges or viewpoints allows us to see what Foucault calls the "swarming" of the disciplinary mechanisms—those mechanisms that can change from locally grounded forces of power confined to particular institutions to far-reaching relationships of power. Citing Foucault (1978), Rouse (1994, p. 107) points out that these networks of power are not static because power circulates and is produced from "one moment to the next." Thus, as I point out in chapter 1, particular viewpoints, stances, and approaches to research in disciplines can assume, over time, "naturalized" and "commonsensical" overtones.

Knowledges and cultures of TCs, then, are never simply there, contained in one discipline or institution or being. Their constitution depends vitally on their constant reenactment and reproduction over time of particular components, including peripheral agents, being aligned in certain ways. Indeed, the role of peripheral agents in TCs is central to establishing and enforcing connections between what a "dominant agent" does and the "fulfillment and frustration of a subordinate agent's desires" (Rouse, 1994, p. 106). It is important to note that notions of dominant and peripheral are always relative and must be understood in relation to the contexts in which they are used. Power, then, is not invested only in the dominant agent but is spread out as a network across a range of socially aligned and coordinated facets that assume dominant or peripheral positions, given the prominence or lack of prominence afforded to power at any given time. Thus, hot topics/debates or new and upcoming areas of research in the field can be seen to assume more power than other areas in the discipline. (Examples of research domains that currently seem to be hot topics include the global spread of English and computer-assisted language learning.) This remains the case until alignments shift and other topics/debates become prominent.

I have argued that enrolled TESOLers should become critically aware of all of these aspects in their socialization process because this awareness is the first step in *countering* what they perceive to be dominant alignments with *alternative* ones. Wartenberg (1990) explains that "countering alignments are a means through which power of a dominant agent within a power relationship can be constrained," whereas alternative alignments indicate that agents have "means of access to the same items that [they] could have access to through the original alignment" (p. 175). Having TESOLers critically reflect on and articulate local and not-so-local ways in which all three alignments—dominant, countering, and alternative—play themselves out in the TESOLers' everyday professional existence moves them toward meta-awareness. Alerting TESOLers to how alignment functions in the various and different textbooks they use in their classrooms, for example, entails their becoming aware of the textbook as a genre unto itself—a point that is important for them to recognize because it enables them "to understand their [textbook's] special language of direct instruction"(Bleich, 1999, p. 17). Getting them to think of textbooks as a genre will encourage them "to remember how and why [the books] are produced, who writes them, who reads them, who sells them, how sales are conducted, and how their kind and style changes" (Bleich, 1999, p. 17).

Making TESOLers aware of the sociopolitical and economic factors shaping the pedagogical materials industry is a step toward recognizing a set of dominant alignments, which is a juncture they have to reach before they can move on to establish an alternative set of alignments. Similar critical reflections and questions can be encouraged for local practices in individual programs and the larger TESOL discipline: Should the divergence between MA-TESOL programs be an issue the larger TC addresses more directly than it currently does? Likewise, isolating particular social practices that potential teachers engage in—both in smaller and larger TCs—encourages questions; for example, how does the TESOLer's individual and collective alignment with and participation in these practices perpetuate or alter certain genres and text types?

Heightening the Metacognitive Skills of Potential (TESOL) Teachers

I turn now to how the meta-awareness of potential teachers might be explicitly and systematically built into existing curricula. I draw on previously addressed aspects of distributed cognition and activity theories.

Making (TESOL) teachers aware of how their thought collectives function as activity systems

Connecting (everyday) actions and goals. One way to alert potential teachers to how their TCs are activity systems of which they are an integral part is by getting them to articulate ways they are sutured into the TCs. Enabling potential teachers to see how their everyday participation in their TCs is tied to their personal goals, which in turn are tied to the (goals of) TCs, is important if they are to discern their location—amid the location and roles of other components—in the TC. Also important is getting them to recognize how the tools in the TC they use—including those they use in their classrooms (textbooks, curricular materials, syllabi)—achieve, with varying success, the goals they set for themselves (or the courses they are teaching). Activity theory posits that objects and tools (Nardi, 1996) are used to target particular goals, that actions are conscious (one has a goal in mind), and that different actions may be undertaken to meet the same goal (with some actions being more fruitful than others). As Leont'ev says, "a person may have the object of obtaining food, but to do so he must carry out actions not immediately directed at obtaining food. . . . His goal may be to make a hunting weapon. Does he subsequently use the weapon he made, or does he pass it on to someone else and receive a portion of the total catch? In both cases, that which energizes his activity and that to which his action is directed do not [necessarily have to] coincide" (quoted in Nardi, 1996, p. 74).

Thus, there does not have to be a direct one-to-one relationship between actions and goals in an activity system. A variety of seemingly unrelated, indirect actions can cumulatively percolate toward achieving directly or indirectly related goals. Having potential TESOLers, for instance, identify some ways in which this process occurs in their TCs—how their everyday actions of attending classes and completing their assignments are tied to their larger goals of becoming EFL/ESL teachers, that the tools (assignments, readings, presentations, theses) they use toward reaching their goals may or may not be direct mediators between themselves and their TESOL worlds—is important for their sense of location in their TCs. The tools that teachers use influence their cognitions and are influenced by a range of factors, including local constraints, the availability and choice of tools at the time, and the general preference of choosing one tool over others. For instance, an MA-TESOL student teacher may, in a program that offers a choice between comprehensive exams and a thesis, decide to do a thesis. Because successful completion of one of these two tools is required for graduation, and because enrolled TESOLers typically want to graduate, these tools are directly tied to student goals. The extra work a TESOLer might do, on the other hand—tutoring an ESL child in her spare time, when it is not a requirement for her program—would be an example of a tool that is (relatively) indirectly tied to her MA-TESOL degree (but enhances her abilities as an ESL teacher).

Also important is heightening the awareness of potential teachers to how choice is built into their everyday actions. Making potential TESOLers critically aware, for example, of how they automatically choose to address their written class assignments in standard English—instead of using colloquialisms or the vernacular—is likely to raise important issues that all teachers need to address: that we are making a definite choice when using this variety of language in an academic setting, that we recognize that it yields better results than a nonstandard variety, that we are aware that power is unevenly assigned to different language varieties, that teachers play a role in perpetuating this unequal distribution by upholding the worth of one appropriate variety (Fairclough, 1995), and what can be done to address inequalities. Providing arenas where potential L2 teachers can consciously make such connections and critically reflect on how their choices in the everyday activities of their TC index a variety of nuances about themselves, and how these automatic choices orient them toward using particular tools, is crucial to enhancing their overall meta-awareness.

Connecting actions and cognitions. Equally important is heightening the awareness of potential teachers to how particular events and actions perpetuate certain kinds of cognitions in their TCs. Sensitizing them to how their participation in various activities of their thought collective—including classes, meetings, student conferences, term papers, exams—ultimately stabilizes and perpetuates particular modes of thought is crucial. If, for example, the general thrust of a particular MA-TESOL program is more on intercultural relations in EFL contexts than on teaching methodology, and the classes, curricular materials, and general orientation of the program leans in this direction, then the cognitions of the enrolled TESOLers are likely to be more heightened in this area. Getting potential teachers to become aware of how their cognitions are thus locally shaped by prevailing and dominant modes of thought in their current environment—as I point out in chapter 2—will ultimately help them to see how different cognitions and modes of thought make their way into the larger discipline. It will provide them with a clearer sense of how the collective leaning of groups of scholars toward one research area can contribute to the flowering of specific modes of thought— how various theories of second language development, for instance, are formed, stabilized, or discarded—and how their involvement in their respective TESOL programs ultimately contributes to keeping particular cognitions in the larger discipline in place. Such awareness is likely to reduce the gap between themselves and the theories out there and will allow them to see connections between themselves and the seemingly free-floating cognitions in their TCs.

Having teachers recognize how the activities they are engaged in constitute the context, and how cognition gets distributed across various components in their TCs

Activity theory proposes that the activity itself is the context: "What takes place in an activity system composed of objects, actions, and operations, is the context" (Nardi, 1996, p. 76). Context is not relegated to phenomena external to the individual but is regarded as internal to the person. This viewpoint introduces a unity, an inseparability of thought and activity, where action and thinking are not mutually exclusive. Cognition is seen as distributed across individuals participating in activities and in the tools and artifacts they use when engaged in particular activities. According to Flor and Hutchins (1991), distributed cognition

> is a new branch of cognitive science devoted to the study of: the representation of knowledge both inside the heads of individuals and in the world . . . ; the propagation of knowledge between different individuals and artifacts . . . ; the transformations which external structures undergo when operated on by individuals and artifacts. . . . By studying cognitive phenomena in this fashion it is hoped that an understanding of how intelligence is manifested at the systems level, as opposed to the individual cognitive level, will be obtained. (quoted in Nardi, 1996, p. 77)

In other words, distributed cognition views its minimal unit of analysis as comprising agents, activities, and tools, among other components. Because the system is not relative to an individual but to a distributed collection of interacting people and artifacts, we cannot understand how a system achieves its goals without understanding the coordinated efforts of all the individual agents and their respective tools (Nardi, 1996).

Heightening the awareness of potential teachers to how cognition gets distributed across various components in an MA-TESOL TC (including reading, writing, discussing, seminars, practicums, and assignment practices) and how this distribution is intimately tied to the goals of the TC (namely to produce informed, effective, self-reflective teachers of English) will enable them to see how they and their TC move globally toward their respective goals. It will also allow them to see how cognition gets spread out across and aligned with varied components in the discipline at large, with some clusters of components evolving their own subdiscourses (Gee, 1990) within the TC. Take, for example, the area of second-language writing. Having L2 writing teachers articulate their participation with particular debates in the field (in both TCs—their immediate teacher education programs and the larger discipline) through the classes they teach and the papers they present at conferences will help them see more tangibly how various positions/cognitions regarding debates get distributed across clusters of peoples.

Examples of such debate in L2 writing concern the extent to which the cultural background of the student is relevant to writing instruction (Ramanathan and Atkinson, 1999; Spack, 1997) or a more recent debate regarding feedback on grammar (Ferris, 1999; Truscott, 1999). Getting potential (L2) teachers to position themselves—both in the realms of theory and practice—in these debates will allow them to link various aspects of their individual participation to them; it will also allow them to see how various components of the debate get acted on, responded to, and carried further. Such multifaceted awareness will afford them a more global vision of the field and their position in it.

Having potential teachers recognize persistent and evolving structures in their TCs and having them reflect on their individual and collective roles in the stability and growth of these structures

Establishing connections between persistent text types and TCs. Along with heightening their awareness of how cognitions get distributed in their TCs, we must also make enrolled teachers conscious of the relatively persistent/stable structures (Nardi, 1996) of their TCs. By persistent structures I mean certain ways of talking, including jargon terms, particular artifacts, institutions, tools, disciplinary values, textual forms/genres, registers—components that are reasonably stable and not likely to change quickly. Alerting potential teachers to how various cognitions get rooted in these persistent components and how both cognitions and components are encased in and constitutive of a range of social practices is important if they are to engage in metatalk. Making them aware of how various persistent social practices in TCs keep particular written genres stable (how the social practice of having them write readers' notes, for example, for particular readings in the seminars they take keeps the genre of readers' notes persistent and stable in the TC) or how the practice of submitting and reviewing abstracts (Kaplan et al., 1994) partially sustains the genre of well-written abstracts in the TCs is crucial. Equally important is getting them to see that disciplinary changes occur over time (for example, that changes in social practices/conventions in the scientific discourse community have led to changes in scientific writing [Atkinson, 1998b; Huckin, 1987]). Having them recognize how key textual components—abstracts, proposals, term papers, textbooks, readings, and assignments—are, thus, relatively persistent tools in their TCs, that even slight changes in these tools can have a ripple effect on the general orientation and ecology of the TC, will afford them a more holistic vision of the relative (im)movables in their TCs.

How persistent text types get co-constructed. Encouraging potential teachers to reflect on how they co-construct the different texts they engage in (Wells, 1996) entails getting them to recognize when particular situation types demand specific textual forms. They would do this based on their knowledge of "regular patterns of co-occurrence that exist between particular semiotic properties of the situation and particular choices from the semantic resources that make up the culture's linguistic meaning potential (register) and of the way in which these choices are sequentially deployed in the staged organization of the event (genre)" (Wells, 1999, p. 9). Heightening meta-awareness of such issues is necessary if we want potential L2 teachers not to be constrained by persistent structures, including those that constitute stereotypical class lessons, but to feel empowered to strike out in relevant but different directions that entail rethinking some of the persistent structures with which they contend.

Making teachers conscious of teacher-student discourse. Particular kinds of speech in the TC can be classified under persistent structures as well. Lemke (1988) details ways that certain kinds of responses made by teachers to student contributions do or do not enhance student performance:

Continually to choose the "evaluate" option—whether accepting or rejecting—does much to create a situational context in which right answers will be given priority by students. By contrast, frequently choosing the "extend" option creates a different context—one which emphasizes the collaborative construction of meaning, both in the setting of goals to be aimed for and in the construction of "common knowledge." And the choice of the options which call upon students to justify, explain and exemplify creates another context—one which encourages students critically to examine and evaluate the answers that they make to the questions that interest them and which simultaneously provides an opportunity for their apprenticeship into these "genres of power." (quoted in Wells, 1996, p. 97)

Increasing teachers' self-awareness about the types of feedback they offer their students and alerting them to ways that changes in their utterances can make a difference in the relative success of student performance are important if teachers are to see how persistent and rooted their kind of talk is. As Wells points out, in much of the research in the human sciences the emphasis has been on investigating how activity systems determine ways that actions are operationalized. Concentrating on teacher talk "invites us to consider the converse relationship—how changing the 'operations' by means of which an 'action' is carried out can ultimately change the 'activity system' in which the 'action' is embedded" (Wells, 1996, p. 97). In these small ways teachers can effect changes in education; by cultivating meta-awareness of specific features of their talk, they can transform the persistent, sometimes negative features of their speech into kinds of speech that will elicit better student responses.

Alerting teachers to the perspectivity of all viewpoints. Making potential teachers aware of how they can analyze their TC from a variety of angles (from the individual to the broadest disciplinary levels) and of the ways in which the picture changes depending on the perspective taken (Russell, 1995, p. 56) can only enhance their sense that all viewpoints are perspectival. Getting them to see, for instance, that an anthropological take on TESOL as a discipline would in all likelihood have serious reservations about the spread of English-language literacy across the world, given the slow erosion of local, indigenous languages it might engender (Phillipson, 1992), will afford them insight into how views external to their thought collective might be diametrically opposed to the TC's goals. Therefore, alerting them to the possibility of such views would be a first step in getting them to recognize that what they regard as immovables in the TC can, from another disciplinary point of view, be seen as relatively movable and questionable.

Having teachers articulate explicit connections linking texts, various domains of reference, and various teaching-learning contexts

Making explicit connections among texts. Alerting potential teachers to the general notion of intertextuality, how contexts always harken back to previous or concurrent ones, and the ways that such connections get played out in the various domains of their teacher education existence, is crucial if they are to understand the general web of interconnectedness that they are in and that they help create. As Lemke (1995) points out, "Each community and every subcommunity within it has its own system of intertextuality: its own set of important or valued texts, its own preferred discourses, and particularly its own habits of deciding which texts should be read in the context of which others, and why, and how" (p. 10). Encouraging potential teachers to articulate, among other things, how a "text is not an autonomous or unified object, but a set of relations with other texts" (Leitch, quoted in Porter, 1986, p. 35), and getting them to establish the numerous ways in which their current texts evidence traces of other texts, is central to their schema building. It is also central to their overall understanding of how they contribute to the system of intertextuality that glues the TCs together (Lemke, 1995).

One way to encourage this awareness is by having potential teachers re-create through assigned readings the (partial) context of a debate in the field (for example, the universality of the communicative approach to L2 language teaching) and to anticipate some problems that may arise when transplanting the debate across cultures (Holliday, 1994). Such exercises will help to heighten their sensitivity to particular positions taken in related texts and alert them to ways that texts draw on prior texts for much of their meaning. Likewise, having teachers juxtapose texts from different discourses (examining the rhetorical patterns of texts from different disciplines or different cultures), or juxtapose texts from different historical stages of a discourse (Gee, 1997) (such as comparing features of scientific writing from the 18th century to current scientific articles), or even texts of different authors writing on similar issues (Cazden, 1989), will encourage them to make explicit connections among their intertextual store-houses and domains of reference, thus fostering a level of meta-awareness about textual forms.

Making explicit inter(con)textual connections among teaching-learning contexts. Encouraging teachers to make explicit inter-(con)textual connections between what and how they learn and what and how they teach is crucial to their seeing the constant interplay linking theory, practice, and the individual's evolution as teacher and learner. Having teachers articulate ways that their experiences with a particular language teaching method do or do not comport with what they are reading about, or how their peer-reviewing workshops in their writing classrooms do or do not connect meaningfully with their course readings regarding the same, will give them opportunities to critically position themselves vis-à-vis their experiences in the classroom and what they read. Articulating such connections will heighten their orientational dimension (Lemke, 1995, p. 11) by making them conscious of how they direct their evolving views and meanings to particular audiences while recognizing that these views are located within a "system of different viewpoints available in the community [read TC] toward our topic" (Lemke, 1995, p. 11). What potential teachers draw from their readings and how these readings get translated into what they do in the classroom when teaching index value preferences and stances that commit them to (or dis-associate them from) the politics of their TCs. Making them meta-aware of this bidirectional relationship between theory and practice, between what they read and how they act, between their personal orientations and the larger dynamics of their TCs, is crucial if they are to grasp how "orientational meaning situates us in the realm of textual politics" (Lemke, 1995, p. 11).

Conclusion

Gee (1999) maintains that entry and acceptance into a community (read TC) depend to a large extent on the degree to which the novice has learned the community's social language, thereby developing recognizable social identities. He characterizes a social language as one that "offers speakers or writers distinctive grammatical resources with which they can 'design' their oral and written 'utterances' to accomplish two inter-related things: a) to get recognized by others (and themselves) as enacting a specific socially situated *identity* (that is, to 'come off' as a particular 'kind of person') and b) to get recognized by others (and themselves) as engaged in a specific *activity*" (p. 16).

Clearly, the socialization that teacher education programs offer is oriented toward potential teachers and the developing of their social languages. Through this development they become identifiable as full participants in the TCs, and, as much of this book has discussed, these social languages emerge from and are embedded in specific social practices. Not only is it crucial that potential teachers pick up this social language in their socialization through their individual programs, but it is equally important that they develop a meta-awareness about it for their individual development and growth (Martin, 2001). Although it is important for educators to have acquired the rules of the trade before encouraging meta-awareness about them—indeed Martin (2001) argues that learners need to deal with discourses as discourses before they can be critical of them—it is equally important to keep in mind that adult learners have already acquired a great many of the required discourses before they come to a teacher education program. In fact, their admission into a teacher education program is contingent on their already being partially proficient in the relevant discourses necessary for successful completion of the program.

The kind of meta-awareness that I am promoting is similar to Lemke's (1995) proposition on reflection on *praxis*, namely, adopting a self-reflexive and self-critical attitude that encourages reflection and analysis on the stable and evolving practices of a community, including those practices related to texts, genres, social interaction, and individual participation in their creation and sustenance. Meta-awareness includes getting teachers to view their TC worlds as activity systems that have and reproduce local ideologies that seem "naturalized" or "commonsensical" because they are held in place, in part, by the individual's participation in the various social practices of the collective. Such awareness is crucial if we want aspiring teachers to recognize that the "common sense [or natural] in its ideological dimension is itself an *effect of power*" and that sometimes a "naturalized type tends to be perceived not as that of a particular grouping within the institution but as simply that of the institution itself" (Fairclough, 1989, p. 92, author's emphasis). Such an approach will help all teachers to move beyond the series of oppositions that seem endemic to teacher education (qualitative vs. quantitative research methods, sociolinguistic vs. cognitive approach to language learning, communicative language teaching vs. traditional methods) toward developing a more nuanced, comprehensive, critical theory of practice (Bourdieu, 1991) wherein they address how such oppositions get created and reinforced in the first place.

This kind of meta-awareness can emerge only through deliberate and frequent questioning and analysis of ways in which the various and intricate aspects of socialization shape the potential teachers' identities, as well as ways in which teachers make meaning of these (con)texts. As Lemke maintains, "it is not the texts as objects, nor the speech as verbal text, that makes meaning, but our activity in interacting with these, producing and interpreting them, that makes meaning." Texts do not have meaning; "meanings are relations we make through practices in which we are never the sole participant, never the sole originator of the practice" (1995, pp. 158–159). Certainly, Fleck's definition of thought collectives complements this view: "common understanding and mutual misunderstanding" produce a set of relations and meanings, "a thought structure [*Denkgebilde*]" that belongs simultaneously to nobody in particular and to everybody in general. Getting potential teachers to fully comprehend this fact, making them meta-aware of the different ways their TCs sustain, produce, and evolve meanings within and among their various components, will inevitably alert them to the issues this book has discussed—how all texts harken back to other texts, how the activities teachers are engaged in are a result of local and not-so-local cognitions in their TCs, how their TCs have persistent structures that anchor various and distributed cognitions.

Building a degree of meta-awareness into every course that enrolled L2 teachers take—where they self-consciously focus on and question the various components of their socialization process and their individual participation and contribution—will ulti-mately allow them to view their TCs as "dynamic open systems" (Lemke, 1995, p. 162) whose general balance and stability are par-tially in their hands. This kind of acknowledgment and question-ing of the phenomenon of naturalization has as one of its layers a "commonsensical" approach that needs to be peeled away to reveal its second layer, an *essence* (Fairclough, 1989, p. 92). Cognizant of and as participants in a collective that makes room for and encour-ages such peeling and revealing, TESOLers will ultimately be able to understand that they can collectively and individually respond to and change their TCs, that were it not for the TESOLers them-selves the TCs would not exist. Such awareness can only be empowering.

Appendix A

Kinds of Data Collected from the Two Programs

Written documents

a. course descriptions
b. formal and informal curricular designs
c. syllabi
d. textbooks
e. orientation materials
f. teacher preparation workshop handouts
g. graduate student handbooks
h. acceptance/admission letters sent out to students
i. an exit questionnaire administered to graduating students (see below for questions)

Interviews

Interviews of the following participants lasted between 45 and 90 minutes each:

MA-TESOL at SEU	MA-TESOL at WCU
Chair of English	Chair of Linguistics
Director of Composition	Two ESL coordinators
Director of MA-TESOL	Director of MA-TESOL
Two currently enrolled students	Two currently enrolled students

Themes addressed in interviews with department chairs and program directors in the two programs

History of the program—how it became part of English/ Linguistics
The role it plays in the department
The general strengths of the program

Particular philosophies regarding language teaching
The direction/s the department is headed in
What the primary aim/s of MA-TESOL programs should be
Ways in which the MA-TESOL program gets connected to other departments on campus
Whether a PhD in applied linguistics will affect MA-TESOL

Themes addressed in interviews with program administrative personnel

General focus of the program
Ways the program has evolved historically
Role of general linguistics/literature in the program
How issues related to practicum get worked out
General focus of teaching skills for developing teachers (approaches to teaching language skills)
Teaching areas personnel would like to see improved
Potential changes in the program
Particular philosophies regarding teacher education
Balancing points of emphasis (ESL vs. EFL, K–12 vs. tertiary, oral skills vs. written skills)
Connections to other departments on campus
Primary disciplines informing the programs
Presence of a PhD in applied linguistics

Field notes

Field notes on local contexts in both programs, including class observations; observation of administrative meetings; orientations; and formal and informal discussions with faculty, students, and administrators.

Course requirements

Required courses for the MA-TESOLer at WCU (on the quarter system): Theory of Second Language Acquisition, Research on Second Language Acquisition, Individual and Social Aspects of Bilingualism, The Teaching of English as a Foreign Language, Materials of TESOL, Recent Research and Projects in TESOL,

Practicum in TESOL (3 quarters), Historical Linguistics, Phonetics, Semantics, Phonological Analysis, Grammatical Analysis, Introduction to Syntactic Theory, and other elective courses.

Required courses for the MA-TESOLer at SEU (on the semester system): TESOL Methods and Materials, Second Language Development, Teaching Academic Writing to ESL Students, Teaching ESL Writing through Literature, Special Topics in TESOL (two required: e.g., Multicultural Literacies, Cross-Cultural Communication, Pedagogical Grammar, Research Methods in Applied Linguistics), Introduction to Linguistics, Seminar in Linguistics, Structure of English, Dialectology, and other elective courses.

Exit questionnaire

The following questions were submitted to advanced and graduating students in both programs:

What are some of your overall opinions of the MA-TESOL program?

Which classes did you find most useful? Why?

Which classes could you have done without? Why?

What in the program works really well and what would you like changed? Why?

How do you feel about the teaching experience you got in the program? Which experiences were most useful?

How do you feel about the feedback you received on your teaching? How could this be improved?

In terms of your practical development as a teacher in the program:

Which language teaching skills do you feel you have gained most proficiency in?

Which language teaching skills would you have liked more practice in?

Which language teaching contexts do you feel prepared to handle (please circle all that apply)?

teaching overseas
teaching in a community college
teaching in an intensive English program
teaching in a writing program
teaching K–12
teaching English for specific purposes
other (please specify)

Describe your ideal teaching position. Who are the learners? What are the goals of the course?

Which language teaching skills do you consider yourself to be weakest in? Why?

Other relevant comments:

Appendix B

Selected Topics from Current L1 Freshman Composition Textbooks

Abortion
Affirmative action
Animal experimentation
Animal rights
Bilingual education
Capital punishment
Censorship
Children's rights
Competition
Consumerism
Culture and the curriculum
Cultures in contacts
Defining women's lives
Democracy
Drug testing
Education
Education and empowerment
Education, business, and work
Endangered species
Environment of prejudice
Ethics, justice, and religion
Euthanasia
Family/home
Free speech
Freedom of oppression
Functions of the family
Gay marriages
Gender
Generations

Global warming
Gun control
Guns and public safety
History
History and politics
Idea of a university
Language and literature
Legalizing drugs
Mass media
Melting pot
Money and success
Moralities
Multicultural identities
Myth of the model family
Nature and technology
Nuclear armaments
Our relationship to our natural environment
Politics
Prejudice
Public space
Right to life
Risks of human cloning
Science and technology
Sex education
Sex, gender, and family
Sexual harassment
Sexuality
Single parenthood
Style
Television culture
Testing for drugs
Views about minority voices
Women in the corporate workplace
Women in the military
Women's rights
Working in the world

Notes

Introduction

1. See, e.g., Auerbach (1996), Benesch (1991), and Giroux (1992).
2. Similar to Freeman's study is one by Richards, Ho, and Giblin (1996), who examine how five trainee teachers responded to a short teacher training program. Richards et al. found that teachers interpret their programs in significantly different ways as they attempt to deconstruct their experiences in the light of their "beliefs and assumptions about themselves, about teachers, about teaching, and about learners" (p. 258).
3. Such reflection is supposed to foster the Deweyan characteristics of open-mindedness (the ability to suspend judgment, to consider alternative viewpoints), responsibility (the ownership of consequences for actions), and wholeheartedness (feelings of commitment to continuous professional development) (Vacca et al., 1997).
4. For a comprehensive review on encouraging reflective practice among L1 teachers, see Vacca et al. (1997). Van Maanen (1977) discusses three kinds of teacher reflection: (1) technical reflection, which encourages teachers to address day-to-day problems in their classrooms; (2) practical reflection, which includes thinking of long-term educational goals; and (3) critical reflection, which encourages thinking about ethical dimensions of teaching.
5. Although such stability may in some senses be unfortunate—at least in that it diminishes innovation in writing—it is absolutely essential to ensure continuity and comprehensibility in the transfer of information within and across disciplinary communities. The perpetuation of genres provides conventional solutions, developed over extended periods, to recurring communication problems. If all known genres were

suddenly eradicated, it would simply be necessary to reinvent them because no text is an isolate but exists in the context of previous and co-occurring texts. It is not my purpose to propose a substitute for existing genres but to explore ways that we may disseminate genres with greater efficiency while discouraging slavish imitation of them.

6. By *sociotextual* I mean the mutual co-construction and inseparability of social content and text.

Chapter 1. The Politics of (TESOL) Thought Collectives

1. Other advantages of this interpretation of *discourse community* include (1) its tolerance for a high degree of ambiguity, (2) its ability to take a historical view of communities, and (3) its perception of communities not as "nice neat packages" but as "messy, ill defined and unstable" (Porter, 1992, p. 88).

Chapter 2. The Politics of Local MA-TESOL Programs and Implications for the Larger TC

1. See Ramanathan, Davies, and Schleppegrell (2001). I have drawn on this paper with the kind permission of my coauthors and of *TESOL Quarterly*.

2. Both programs are at research universities and, in that sense, do not represent all ESL-related programs.

3. Davies and I met several times during the year to gather data, conduct interviews, and discuss the ongoing research process. Schleppegrell and I work in the same institution and met at least once a month regarding this project.

4. I interviewed Davies and Schleppegrell—each of whom were at the time of the interviews directors of the two programs—to get their takes on various program-related issues. We typically identified interviewees in terms of what they brought to each program: their extensive teaching and administrative experience, the number of years they had been associated with the program/department, and their historical sense of how their program evolved.

5. Throughout this book I will indicate quotes from interviews

with "FI" (Faculty Interview); the number following the abbreviation represents the transcript number of the specific interview.

6. TAs are sometimes assigned to teach native sections of composition if there are not enough nonnative sections available.

7. The state's Commission on Higher Education mandates that TAs have 18 hours of graduate credit before they can serve as a main teacher in a composition classroom.

8. If the program wants to admit more students than the TA lines allotted to it, it has to borrow TA lines from one of the other strands in the program. Perhaps surprisingly, this has generally not been a problem in the recent past.

9. The course work that WCU TESOLers took in the English department was a sequence of three methods courses, so by moving the methods courses and practicum site (the ESL program) to linguistics, the MA-TESOL program became fully located in the linguistics department.

10. As a matter of fact, the ESL instructors in English were housed in trailers outside the department. Thus, apart from feeling distanced, they were physically removed from the mainstream department as well.

11. This shifting of emphasis may be more likely in one school than another, depending on the larger departmental constraints.

12. Aware of this issue, the directors of both programs advise their students to state in detail on their curricula vitae what their degree consists of, especially in terms of (supervised) teaching experience.

Chapter 3. The Politics of Genres and Text Types

1. In his later work (Swales, 1998), Swales raises the issue of whether the boundaries of a discourse community can be drawn and wonders whether it might be more appropriate to see the discourse community of a discipline as radiating out in concentric circles to the larger department, the school, and the social community.

2. Teaching observation reports exemplify a genre that has worked successfully in the MA-TESOL programs of which I have been a part. I do not, by any means, intend to imply that these texts are used across TESOL programs or that they ought to be.

3. This point is underscored in Swales's findings on research articles in the sciences. Based on an analysis of 16 articles each in physics, biology, medicine, and the social sciences, Swales (1990) identifies four common moves and submoves (read textual forms) in the introductory sections of papers:

   Move 1: Establishing the field
   [by] showing centrality
   stating current knowledge
   ascribing key characteristics
   Move 2: Summarizing previous research
   Move 3: Preparing for present research
   Move 4: Introducing present research
   [by] giving the purpose
   describing present research

   Although this breakdown has been criticized as too simple (Cookes, 1986) because it does not account for multiple embeddings within individual moves, the point is that these moves are units of textual forms that related TCs and authors in those communities use to communicate their research and to further their respective goals.

4. There is no question that e-mail communication has engendered other kinds of changes—e.g., the use of visual shorthand commentary such as emoticons—e.g., :-) ;-) :-(—as well as a whole new lexicon ("flaming") and a host of stylistic changes not yet carefully examined or thoroughly understood. Some of these changes are, no doubt, specific to particular discourse communities.

5. See, e.g., Gould and Lewontin (1970). Selzer's edited volume *Understanding Scientific Prose* (1993) is devoted to addressing rhetorically related issues in this one article.

Chapter 4. The Politics of Written Knowledge

1. I do not offer definitions of *audience* or *voice* per se partly because (1) these terms have already been variously defined in rhetoric research and (2) defining these terms is not as central to the present discussion as are the inductive/problematic ways in which they are presented in several writing textbooks. Not only are these terms difficult for nonnative student writers, as I have argued in this chapter, but many L1 writing researchers have also raised serious questions about traditional textbook approaches to these notions. For discussions of these terms, see Ede and Lunsford (1984), Kroll (1984), Park (1982, 1986), Porter (1986), and Purves (1988).

References

Agger, B. (1992). *Cultural studies as critical theory*. Washington, D.C.: Falmer Press.

Alasuutari, P. (1995). *Researching culture: Qualitative method and cultural studies*. Thousand Oaks, CA: Sage.

Allwright, D., and Bailey, K. (1991). *Focus on the language classroom*. New York: Cambridge University Press.

Alvesson, M. (1993). *Cultural perspectives on organizations*. New York: Cambridge University Press.

Anderson, B. (1991). *Imagined communities*. New York: Verso.

Apple, M. (1990). *Ideology and curriculum*. New York: Routledge.

Apple, M., and Christian-Smith, L. (Eds.) (1991). *The politics of the textbook*. New York: Routledge.

Aronowitz, S., and Giroux, H. (1985). *Education under siege: The conservative, liberal, and radical debate over schooling*. South Hadley, MA: Bergin and Garvey.

Aronowitz, S., and Giroux, H. (1993). *Education still under siege*. Westport, CT: Bergin and Garvey.

Atkinson, D. (1998a). A critical approach to critical thinking in TESOL. *TESOL Quarterly* 31(1): 71–94.

Atkinson, D. (1998b). *Scientific discourse in sociohistorical context: The philosophical transactions of the Royal Society of London, 1675–1975*. Mahwah, NJ: Lawrence Erlbaum.

Atkinson, D., and Ramanathan, V. (1995). "Cultures of writing": An ethnographic comparison of L1 and L2 university writing/language programs. *TESOL Quarterly* 29(3): 539–568.

Atkinson, P. (1992). *Understanding ethnographic texts*. Newbury Park, CA: Sage.

Auerbach, E. (1996). *Adult ESL/literacy from the community to the community: A guidebook for participatory literacy training*. Mahwah, NJ: Lawrence Erlbaum.

Bailey, K., and Nunan, D. (Eds.) (1996). *Voices from the language classroom*. Cambridge, UK: Cambridge University Press.

Bakhtin, M. (1986). *Speech genres and other late essays* (V. W. McGee, Trans.). Austin: University of Texas Press.

Barnet, S., and Bedau, H. (1993, 1999, 2002). *Current issues and enduring questions: A guide to critical thinking and argument with readings*. Boston: Bedford/St. Martin's.

Barthes, R. (1988). The death of the author. In D. Lodge (Ed.), *Modern criticism and theory* (pp. 166–172). New York: Longman.

Bateson, G. (1972). Forms, substance, and difference. In *Steps to the ecology of mind*. New York: Ballantine.

Bazerman, C. (1988). *Shaping written knowledge: The genre and activity of the experimental article in science*. Madison: University of Wisconsin Press.

Becher, T. (1981). Toward a definition of disciplinary cultures. *Studies in Higher Education* 6(2): 109–122.

Benesch, S. (Ed.) (1991). *ESL in America: Myths and possibilities*. Portsmouth, NH: Boynton/Cook.

Benesch, S. (1993). ESL ideology and the politics of pragmatism. *TESOL Quarterly* 27: 705–717.

Benesch, S. (2001). *Critical English for academic purposes: Theory, politics, and practice*. Mahwah, NJ: Lawrence Erlbaum.

Berger, P., and Luckmann, T. (1966). *The social construction of reality: A treatise on the sociology of knowledge*. Garden City, NY: Doubleday.

Berkenkotter, C., and Huckin, T. (1993). Rethinking genre from a sociocognitive perspective. *Written Communication* 10(4): 475–509.

Berlin, J. (1987). *Rhetoric and reality: Writing instruction in American colleges, 1950–1985*. Carbondale, IL: Southern Illinois University Press.

Berman, R., and Slobin, D. (Eds.) (1994). *Relating events in narrative: A crosslinguistic development study*. Hillsdale, NJ: Lawrence Erlbaum.

Bizzell, P. (1992). *Academic discourse and critical consciousness*. Pittsburgh, PA: University of Pittsburgh Press.

Blanton, L. (1998). Discourse, artifacts, and the Ozarks: Understanding academic literacy. In V. Zamel and R. Spacks (Eds.), *Negotiating academic literacies*. Mahwah, NJ: Lawrence Erlbaum.

Bleich, D. (1999). In case of fire, throw in (what to do with textbooks once you switch to source books). In X. L. Gale and F. Gale (Eds.), *Re(visioning) composition textbooks* (pp. 15–42). Albany, NY: State University of New York Press.

Bourdieu, P. (1991). *Language and symbolic power*. Cambridge, MA: Harvard University Press.

Brandt, D. (1986). Toward an understanding of context in composition. *Written Communication* 3: 139–157.

Brannon, L. (1995). (Dis)missing compulsory first-year composition. In J. Petraglia (Ed.), *Reconceiving writing, rethinking writing instruction* (pp. 239–248). Mahwah, NJ: Lawrence Erlbaum.

Brown, J., Collins, A., and Duguid, P. (1989). Situated cognition and the culture of learning. *Education Researcher* 18: 32–42.

Butterfield, E., and Nelson, G. (1991). Promoting positive transfer of different types. *Cognition and Instruction* 8: 69–102.

Campbell, D. (1996). Can we overcome worldview incommensurability/relativity in trying to understand each other? In R. Jessor, A. Colby, and R. Schweder (Eds.), *Ethnography and human development* (pp. 153–172). Chicago: University of Chicago Press.

Canagarajah, S. (1993). Critical ethnography of a Sri Lankan classroom: Ambiguities in student opposition to reproduction in ESOL. *TESOL Quarterly* 27: 601–626.

Canagarajah, S. (2001). Critical academic writing and multilingual students. Unpublished manuscript.

Carnegie Task Force on Teaching as a Profession (1986). *A nation prepared: Teachers for the 21st century*. New York: Carnegie Forum on Education and Economy.

Cazden, C. (1989). Contributions of the Bakhtin circle to "communicative competence." *Applied Linguistics* 10(2): 116–127.

Cedarblom, J., and Paulsen, D. (1987). *Critical reasoning*. Belmont, CA: Wadsworth.

Christie, F. (1993). The "received" tradition of literacy teaching: The decline of rhetoric and corruption of grammar. In B. Green

(Ed.), *The insistence of the letter: Literacy studies and curriculum theorizing* (pp. 75–106). London: Falmer Press.

Coe, R. (1987). An apology for form; or, who took the form out of the process? *College English* 49: 13–28.

Coe, R. (1994). Teaching genre as a process. In A. Freedman and P. Medway (Eds.), *Learning and teaching genre* (pp. 157–169). Portsmouth, NH: Boynton/Cook.

Cole, M., Engestrom, Y., and Vasquez, O. (1997). Introduction. In M. Cole, Y. Engestrom, and O. Vasquez (Eds.), *Mind, culture, and activity* (pp. 1–21). Cambridge, UK: Cambridge University Press.

Cole, M., and Wertsch, J. (1996). *Contemporary implications of Vygotsky and Luria.* Worcester, MA: Clark University Press.

College Board (1983). *Academic preparation for college: What students need to know and be able to do.* New York: College Entrance Examination Board.

Collins, A. (1991). Cognitive apprenticeship and instructional technology. In L. Idol and B. Jones (Eds.), *Educational values and cognitive instruction: Implications for reform* (pp. 121–138). Hillsdale, NJ: Lawrence Erlbaum.

Commission on the Humanities (1980). *The humanities in American life.* Berkeley, CA: University of California Press.

Connor, U., and Kaplan, R. B. (Eds.) (1987). *Writing across languages: Analyses of L2 text.* Reading, MA: Addison-Wesley.

Cookes, G. (1986). Towards a validated analysis of scientific text structure. *Applied Linguistics* 7(1): 57–70.

Cope, B., and Kalantzis, M. (1993). *The powers of literacy: A genre approach to teaching writing.* Pittsburgh, PA: University of Pittsburgh Press.

Cronin, B. (1981). The need for a theory of citing. *Journal of Documentation* 37(1): 16–24.

Davies, C. A. (1999). *Reflexive ethnography: A guide to researching selves and others.* London: Routledge.

Davies, C. E. (1996). *Discourse communities in the linguistic ecology of an American university.* Chicago, IL: American Association of Applied Linguistics.

deBono, E. (1983). The direct teaching of critical thinking. *Phi Delta Kappan* 65: 703–708.

Delpit, L. (1988). The silenced dialogue: Power and pedagogy in educating other people's children. *Harvard Educational Review* 58: 280–298.

Dewey, J. (1966). *Education and democracy.* New York: Free Press.

Durkheim, E. (1915). *The elementary forms of religious life.* London: George Allen and Unwin.

Eagleton, T. (1988). Capitalism, modernism, and postmodernism. In D. Lodge (Ed.), *Modern criticism and theory* (pp. 384–398). New York: Longman.

Eckert, P., and McConnell-Ginet, S. (1992). Think practically and look locally: Language and gender as community-based practice. *Annual Review of Anthropology* 21: 461–490.

Ede, L., and Lunsford, A. (1984). Audience addressed/audience invoiced: The role of audience in composition theory and pedagogy. *College Composition and Communication* 35: 155–171.

Eggington, W. (1987). Written academic discourse in Korean: Implications for effective communications. In U. Connor and R. B. Kaplan (Eds.), *Writing across languages: Analysis of L2 text* (pp. 153–168). Reading, MA: Addison-Wesley.

Ennis, R. (1962). A concept of critical thinking. *Harvard Educational Review* 32: 81–111.

Ennis, R. (1981). Eight fallacies in Bloom's taxonomy. *Philosophy of education 1980: Proceedings of the thirty-sixth annual meeting of the Philosophy of Education Society.* Normal, IL: Philosophy of Education Society.

Ennis, R. (1985). Critical thinking and the curriculum. *National Forum* 65: 28–31.

Ennis, R. (1987). A conception of critical thinking—with some curriculum suggestions. *American Philosophical Association Newsletter on the Teaching of Philosophy,* pp. 1–5.

Ennis, R., and Millman, J. (1985a). *Cornell critical thinking test, level x.* Pacific Grove, CA: Midwest Publications.

Ennis, R., and Millman, J. (1985b). *Cornell critical thinking test, level z.* Pacific Grove, CA: Midwest Publications.

Evans, J. (1982). *The psychology of deductive reasoning.* London: Routledge and Kegan Paul.

Fahnestock, J., and Secor, M. (1991). *A rhetoric of argument.* New York: McGraw-Hill.

Fairclough, N. (1989). *Language and power.* New York: Longman.

Fairclough, N. (1992). *Critical language awareness.* New York: Longman.

Fairclough, N. (1995). *Critical discourse analysis: The critical study of language.* London: Longman.

Ferris, D. (1994). Rhetorical strategies in student persuasive writing: Differences between native and non-native English speakers. *Research in the Teaching of English* 27: 222–251.

Ferris, D. (1999). The case for grammar correction in L2 writing classes: A response to Truscott. *Journal of Second Language Writing* 8(1): 1–11.

Ferris, D., and Hedgcock, J. (1998). *Teaching ESL composition: Purpose, process, and practice.* Mahwah, NJ: Lawrence Erlbaum.

Fleck, L. (1981). *Genesis and the development of a scientific fact.* Chicago: University of Chicago Press.

Flor, N., and Hutchins, S. (1991). Analyzing distributed cognition in software teams: A case study of team programming during perfective software maintenance. In J. Koenemann-Belliveau, J. G. Moher, and S. P. Robertson (Eds.), *Proceedings of the fourth annual workshop on empirical studies of programmers* (pp. 36–59). Norwood, NJ: Ablex.

Foucault, M. (1972). *The archaeology of knowledge* (A. M. Sheridan Smith, Trans.). New York: Pantheon.

Foucault, M. (1978). *The history of sexuality* (R. Hurley, Trans.). New York: Pantheon.

Fowler, R. (1982). *Literature as social discourse: The practice of linguistic criticism.* Bloomington, IN: Indiana University Press.

Fox, H. (1994). *Listening to the world: Cultural issues in academic writing.* Urbana, IL: National Council of Teachers in English.

Freedman, A. (1995). The what, where, why, and how of classroom genres. In J. Petraglia (Ed.), *Reconceiving writing, rethinking writing instruction* (pp. 121–144). Mahwah, NJ: Lawrence Erlbaum.

Freeman, D. (1996). Renaming experience/reconstructing practice: Developing new understandings of teaching. In D. Freeman and J. Richards (Eds.), *Teacher learning in language teaching* (pp. 221–241). Cambridge, UK: Cambridge University Press.

Freeman, D., and Johnson, D. (1998). Reconceptualizing the knowledge-base of language teacher education. *TESOL Quarterly* 32(3): 417.

Fuerstein, R., Jensen, M., Hoffman, M., and Rand, Y. (1985). Instrumental enrichment program for cognitive modifiability: Theory and practice. In J. W. Segal, S. F. Chipman, and R. Glaser (Eds.), *Thinking and learning skills: Relating instruction to research* (pp. 42–82). Hillsdale, NJ: Lawrence Erlbaum.

Futrell, M. H. (1987). A message long overdue. *Education Week* 7(14): 9.

Gee, J. P. (1990). *Social linguistics and literacies: Ideologies in discourses.* Philadelphia: Falmer Press.

Gee, J. P. (1997). Meanings in discourses: Coordinating and being coordinated. In A. Luke and S. Muspratt (Eds.), *Constructing critical literacies: Teaching and learning textual practices* (pp. 273–302). Cresskill, NJ: Hampton Press.

Gee, J. P. (1999). Learning language as a matter of learning social languages within discourses. Paper presented at the College Composition and Communication Conference, Atlanta, GA.

Geertz, C. (2000). *Local knowledge: Further essays in interpretive anthropology* (3d ed.). New York: Basic Books.

Giddens, A. (1979). *Central problems in social theory.* Berkeley, CA: University of California Press.

Gilbert, G. N., and Mulkay, M. (1984). *Opening Pandora's box: A sociological analysis of scientists' discourse.* New York: Cambridge University Press.

Giroux, H. (1992). *Border crossings: Cultural workers and the politics of education.* New York: Routledge.

Glaser, R. (1984). Education and thinking: The role of knowledge. *American Psychologist* 39(2): 93–104.

Goody, E. N. (1989). Learning, apprenticeship, and the division of labor. In M. Coy (Ed.), *Apprenticeship: From theory to method and back again.* Albany, NY: State University of New York Press.

Gould, S., and Lewontin, R. (1970). *The sprandels of San Marco and the Panglossian paradigm: A critique of the adaptionist programme.* London: Proceedings of the Royal Society of London.

Govardhan, A., Nayar, B., and Sheorey, R. (1999). Do U.S. MA-TESOL programs prepare students to teach abroad? *TESOL Quarterly* 33(1): 114–125.

Gramsci, A. (1971). *Selections from the prison notebooks* (Q. Hoare and G. N. Smith, Eds. and Trans.). London: Lawrence and Wishart.

Green, J. L., and Harker, J. O. (1983). *Multiple perspectives on the analyses of classroom discourse.* Norwood, NJ: Ablex.

Greenberg, R. B. (1994). *Contexts and communities: Rhetorical approaches to reading, writing, and research.* New York: Macmillan.

Greenfield, L. (1987). Teaching thinking through problem solving. In J. Stice (Ed.), Developing critical thinking and problem solving abilities (pp. 5–22). San Francisco: Jossey-Bass.

Hammersley, M., and Atkinson, P. (1983). *Ethnography: Principles in practices.* London: Tavistock.

Harris, J. (1990). *Expressive discourse.* Dallas, TX: Southern Methodist University Press.

Heath, S. B. (1983). *Ways with words.* New York: Cambridge University Press.

Heath, S. B. (1985). Literacy or literate skills: Considerations of ESL/EFL learners. In J. P. Larson, E. Judd, and D. Messerschmitt (Eds.), *On TESOL '84* (pp. 15–28). Washington, D.C.: TESOL.

Hedgcock, J. (2002). To appear. Towards a socioliterate approach to L2 teacher education. *Modern Language Journal* 86(3).

Hinds, J. (1987). *Reader vs. writer responsibility: A new typology.* Reading, MA: Addison-Wesley.

Holliday, A. (1994). *Appropriate methodology and social context.* New York: Cambridge University Press.

Holmes Group (1986). *Tomorrow's teachers.* East Lansing, MI: Author.

Horner, B. (1997). Students, authorship, and the work of composition. *College English* 59(5): 505–529.

Huckin, T. (1987). Surprise value in scientific discourse. Paper presented at the College Composition and Communication Conference, Atlanta, GA.

Hunt, R. (1994). Speech genres, writing genres, school genres, and computer games. In A. Medway and P. Medway (Eds.), *Learning and teaching genre* (pp. 243–262). Portsmouth, NH: Boynton/Cook.

Inghileri, M. (1989). Learning to mean as a symbolic and social process: The story of ESL writers. *Discourse Processes* 12: 391–411.

Johns, A. (1995). Genre and pedagogical purposes. *Journal of Second Language Writing* 4(2): 181–190.

Johnson, R. (1992). Critical reasoning and informal logic. In R. Talaska (Ed.), *Critical reasoning in contemporary culture* (pp. 69–88). Albany, NY: State University of New York Press.

Kamberelis, G. (1995). Genre as institutionally informed social practice. *Journal of Contemporary Legal Issues* 6: 115–170.

Kaplan, R. B. (1966). Cultural thought patterns in intercultural education. *Language Learning* 16: 1–20.

Kaplan, R. B., Cantor, S., Hagstrom, C., Kamhi-Stein, L., Shiotani, Y., and Zimmerman, C. (1994). On abstract writing. *Text* 14(3): 401–426.

Kellerman, E. (Ed.) (1995). Crosslinguistic influence: Transfer to nowhere. *Annual Review of Applied Linguistics*. New York: Cambridge University Press.

Kennedy, M., Fisher, M., and Ennis, R. (1991). Critical thinking: Literature review and needed research. In L. Idol and B. F. Jones (Eds.), *Educational values and cognitive instruction: Implications for reform* (pp. 11–40). Hillsdale, NJ: Lawrence Erlbaum.

Killingsworth, M. J., and Gilbertson, M. K. (1992). *Signs, genres, and communities in technical communication*. Amityville, NJ: Baywood.

Kirsch, G., and Roen, D. (Eds.) (1990). *A sense of audience in written communication*. Newbury Park, CA: Sage.

Hodge, R. and Kress, G. (1979). *Language as ideology*. Boston, MA: Routledge and Kegan Paul.

Kroll, B. (1984). Writing for readers: Three perspectives on audience. *College Composition and Communication* 35: 172–185.

Latour, B. (1986). *Laboratory life: The construction of scientific facts.* Princeton: Princeton University Press.

Lave, J. (1988). *Cognition in practice: Mind, mathematics, and culture in everyday life.* New York: Cambridge University Press.

Lave, J., and Wenger, E. (1991). *Situated learning.* New York: Cambridge University Press.

Leitch, V. (1983). *Deconstructive criticism.* Ithaca, NY: Cornell University Press.

Lemke, J. (1988). Genres, semantics, and classroom education. *Linguistics and Education* 1: 81–99.

Lemke, J. (1995). *Textual politics: Discourses and social dynamics.* Bristol, PA: Taylor and Francis.

Lentricchia, F., and McLaughlin, T. (Eds.) (1987). *Critical terms for literary study.* Chicago: University of Chicago Press.

Leont'ev, A. (1959). *Problems in the development of the mind.* Moscow: Moscow University Press.

Lipman, M. (1982). Philosophy for children. *Thinking* 3: 35–44.

Luke, A. (1988). *Literacy, textbooks, and ideology.* London: Falmer Press.

Luria, A. R. (1968). *Speech and development of mental processes in the child: An experimental investigation* (J. Simon, Ed.; O. Kovsac and J. Simon, Trans.). London: Staples Press.

Lutz, F. (1981). Ethnography: The holistic approach to understanding schooling. In J. Green and C. Wallat (Eds.), *Ethnography in educational settings.* Norwood, NJ: Ablex.

MacDonald, S. (1987). Problem definition in academic writing. *College English* 49(3): 315–331.

Mangelsdorf, K., Roen, D., and Taylor, V. (1990). ESL students' use of audience. In G. Kirsch and D. Roen (Eds.), *A sense of written communication* (pp. 231–245). Newbury Park, CA: Sage.

Mannheim, K. (1952). Historicism. In P. Kecskemeti (Ed.), *Essays on the sociology of knowledge.* London: Routledge and Kegan Paul.

Marcus, G. (1988). *Ethnography through thick and thin.* Princeton, NJ: Princeton University Press.

Marcus, G., and Fisher, M. J. M. (1986). *Anthropology and cultural critique: An experimental moment in the human sciences.* Chicago, IL: University of Chicago Press.

Martin, J. R. (2001). Writing history: Construing time and value in the discourse of the past. In M. Schleppegrell and C. Colombi (Eds.), *Developing advanced literacy*. Mahwah, NJ: Lawrence Erlbaum.

McCarthy, D. (1996). *Knowledge as culture*. New York: Routledge.

McLaren, P. (1989). *Life in schools*. New York: Longman.

McPeck, J. (1981). *Critical thinking and education*. New York: St. Martin's.

McPeck, J. (1990). *Teaching critical thinking: Dialogue and dialectic*. New York: Routledge.

Meeker, M. (1969). *The structure of intellect: Its interpretation and uses*. Columbus, OH: Charles E. Merrill.

Michaels, S. (1981). "Sharing time": Children's narrative styles and differential access to literacy. *Language in Society* 10(3): 423–442.

Miller, C. (1984). Genre as social action. *Quarterly Journal of Speech* 70: 151–167.

Miller, R. K. (1998). *The informed argument: A multidisciplinary reader and guide* (5th ed.). Ft. Worth, TX: Harcourt Brace.

Myers, F. (1988). Locating ethnographic practice: Romance, reality, and politics in the outback. *American Ethnologist* 15(4): 609–624.

Nardi, B. (1996). *Context and consciousness: Activity theory and human computer interaction*. Cambridge, MA: MIT Press.

Nelson, B. K. (1981). Hierarchy, utility, and fallacy in Bloom's taxonomy. In *The conference proceedings of the Philosophy of Education 1980* (pp. 260–268). Normal, IL: Philosophy of Education Society.

Nickerson, R. S. (1984). Kinds of thinking taught in current programs. *Educational Leadership* 42(1): 26–36.

Nickerson, R. S. (1987). Why teach thinking? In J. B. Baron and R. J. Sternberg (Eds.), *Teaching thinking skills* (pp. 27–37). New York: Freeman.

Norris, S. (1985). Synthesis of research on critical thinking. *Educational Leadership* 43: 40–45.

Nunan, D. (Ed.) (1992). *Collaborative language learning and teaching*. New York: Cambridge University Press.

Ochs, E. (1988). *Culture and language development: Language acqui-*

sition and language socialization in a Samoan village. New York: Cambridge University Press.

Ochs, E., Schegloff, E., and Thompson, S. (1996). *Interaction and grammar.* New York: Cambridge University Press.

Park, D. (1982). The meanings of "audience." *College English* 44: 247–257.

Park, D. (1986). Analyzing audiences. *College Composition and Communication* 37: 478–487.

Paul, R. W. (1985). Critical thinking research: A response to Stephen Norris. *Educational Leadership* 44: 46.

Penrose, A., and Geisler, C. (1994). Reading and writing without authority. *College Composition and Communication* 45(4): 505–520.

Perryman, M. (Ed.) (1994). *Altered states: Postmodernism, politics, and culture.* London: Lawrence and Wishart.

Petraglia, J. (Ed.) (1995). *Reconceiving writing, rethinking writing instruction.* Mahwah, NJ: Lawrence Erlbaum.

Phillipson, R. (1992). *Linguistic imperialism.* Oxford: Oxford University Press.

Porter, J. (1986). Intertextuality and the discourse community. *Rhetoric Review* 5: 34–47.

Porter, J. (1992). *Audience and rhetoric: An archeological composition of the discourse community.* Englewood Cliffs, NJ: Prentice-Hall.

Prior, P. (1995). Redefining the task: An ethnographic examination of writing and response in graduate seminars. In D. Belcher and G. Braine (Eds.), *Academic writing in a second language.* Norwood, NJ: Ablex.

Purves, A. (1988). *Writing across languages and cultures: Issues in contrastive rhetoric.* Newbury Park, CA: Sage.

Rafoth, B. (1990). The concept of discourse community: Descriptive and explanatory adequacy. In G. Kirsch and D. Roen (Eds.), *A sense of audience in written communication* (pp. 140–152). Newbury Park, CA: Sage.

Raimes, A. (1991). Out of the woods: Emerging traditions in the teaching of writing. *TESOL Quarterly* 25: 407–430.

Ramage, J. D., and Bean, J. C. (1995). *Writing arguments: A rhetoric with readings* (3d ed). New York: Macmillan.

Ramanathan, V. (1997). *Alzheimer's discourse: Some sociolinguistic dimensions.* Mahwah, NJ: Lawrence Erlbaum.

Ramanathan, V. (1999). English is here to stay: A critical look at institutional and educational practices in India. *TESOL Quarterly* 33(2): 211–231.

Ramanathan, V. (2001). Enhancing the critical edge in (L2) teacher-education: Some perspectives in advanced literacy. In M. Schleppegrell and C. Colombi (Eds.), *Developing advanced literacy: Meaning with power.* Mahwah, NJ: Lawrence Erlbaum.

Ramanathan, V., and Atkinson, D. (1999). Individualism, academic writing, and ESL writers. *Journal of Second Language Writing* 8(1): 45–75.

Ramanathan, V., Davies, C., and Schleppegrell, M. (2001). A naturalistic inquiry into the cultures of two divergent MA-TESOL programs: Implications for TESOL." *TESOL Quarterly* 35(2): 279–305.

Ramanathan, V. and Kaplan, R. B. (1996a). Audience and voice in current composition textbooks: Implications for L2 student-writers. *Journal of Second Language Writing* 5(1): 21–34.

Ramanathan, V., and Kaplan, R. B. (1996b). Some problematic channels in the teaching of critical thinking in current L1 composition text-books: Implications for L2 student-writers. *Issues in Applied Linguistics* 7: 225–249.

Ramanathan, V., and Kaplan, R. B. (2000). Genres, authors, and discourse communities: Theory and practice for (L1 and) L2 writing instructors. *Journal of Second Language Writing* 9(2): 171–191.

Ramanathan-Abbott, V. (1993). An examination of the relationship between social practices and the comprehension of narratives. *Text* 13: 117–141.

Resnick, L. (1990). Literacy in school and out. *Daedalus* 119(2): 169–185.

Richards, J., Ho, B., and Giblin, K. (1996). Learning how to teach in the RSA certificate. In D. Freeman and J. Richards (Eds.), *Teacher learning in language teaching* (pp. 242–259). Cambridge, UK: Cambridge University Press.

Richards, J., and Lockhart, C. (1994). *Reflective teaching in second language classrooms.* New York: Cambridge University Press.

Richards, J., and Lockhart, C. (1996). *Reflective teaching through dialogic inquiry*. New York: Cambridge University Press.

Rogoff, B., and Lave, J. (Eds.) (1984). *Everyday cognition*. Cambridge, MA: Harvard University Press.

Rorty, R. (1995). Does academic freedom have philosophical presuppositions? *Academe* (Nov.–Dec.): 52–56.

Ross, J. D., and Ross, C. M. (1976). *Ross test of higher cognitive processes*. Novato, CA: Academic Therapy Publications.

Rottenberg, A. (1994). *Elements of argument* (4th ed.). Boston: Bedford/St. Martin's.

Rottenberg, A. (2000). *Elements of argument* (6th ed.). Boston: Bedford/St. Martin's.

Rouse, J. (1994). Power/knowledge. In Gary Gutting (Ed.), *The Cambridge companion to Foucault*. Cambridge, UK: Cambridge University Press.

Rubenstein, M., and Firstenberg, I. (1987). Tools for thinking. In J. Stice (Ed.), *Developing critical thinking and problem-solving abilities* (pp. 23–36). San Francisco: Jossey-Bass.

Russell, D. (1995). *Activity theory and its implications for writing*. Mahwah, NJ: Lawrence Erlbaum.

Said, E. (1988). Crisis [in Orientalism]. In D. Lodge (Ed.), *Modern criticism and theory* (pp. 295–309). New York: Longman.

Saloman, G. (Ed.) (1993). *Distributed cognitions*. New York: Cambridge University Press.

Schleppegrell, M. (1997). Teacher research through dialogic inquiry. *Canadian Modern Language Review* 54(1): 68–83.

Schleppegrell, M. (2001). Challenges in teacher-training. In G. Bräuer (Ed.), *Pedagogy of language learning in higher education: an introduction*. Westport, CT: Ablex, 2001.

Schleppegrell, M. and Colombi, C. (2002). *Developing advanced literacy*. Mahwah, NJ: Lawrence Erlbaum.

Scollon, R. (1991). *Eight legs and one elbow: Stance and structure in Chinese English compositions*. Banff, AK: International Reading Association.

Scollon, S. (1999). Not to waste words or students: Confucian and Socratic discourse in the tertiary classroom. In E. Hinkel (Ed.),

Culture in second language teaching and learning. Cambridge, UK: Cambridge University Press.

Scollon, R., and Scollon, S. (1981). *Narrative, literacy, and face in interethnic communication.* Norwood, NJ: Ablex.

Scriven, M. (1980). The philosophic and pragmatic significance of informal logic. In A. Blair and R. Johnson (Eds.), *Informal logic: The first international symposium* (pp. 147–160). Inverness, CA: Edgepress.

Scriven., M. (1992). Evaluation and critical reasoning: Logic's last frontier? In R. Talaska (Ed.), *Critical reasoning in contemporary culture* (pp. 353–370). Albany, NY: State University of New York Press.

Siegal, H. (1990). McPeck, informal logic, and the nature of critical thinking. In J. McPeck (Ed.), *Teaching critical thinking* (pp. 75–85). New York: Routledge.

Selzer, J. (1993). *Understanding scientific prose.* Madison: University of Wisconsin Press.

Seyler, D. (1991). *Read, reason, write.* New York: McGraw-Hill.

Shipman, V. (1983). *New Jersey test of reasoning skills.* Upper Montclair College: Upper Montclair, NJ, Test Division.

Shor, I. (1993). *Empowering education: Critical thinking for social change.* Chicago: University of Chicago Press.

Shor, I., and Freire, P. (1987). *A pedagogy for liberation: Dialogues on transforming education.* South Hadley, MA: Bergin and Garvey.

Shore, B. (1996). *Culture in mind.* Oxford: Oxford University Press.

Simpson, D., and Jackson, M. (1997). *Educational reform: A Deweyan perspective.* New York: Garland.

Snow, M. (2000). *Implementing the ESL standards through teacher education.* Baltimore, MD: TESOL.

Spack, R. (1997). The rhetorical construction of multilingual students. *TESOL Quarterly* 31: 765–774.

Stehr, N. (1992). Experts, counsellors, and advisors. In N. Stehr and R. Ericson (Eds.), *The culture and power of knowledge: Inquiries into contemporary society* (pp. 107–155). Berlin: Walter de Gruyter.

Stehr, N., and Ericson, R. (Eds.). (1992). *The culture and power of knowledge: Inquiries into contemporary society.* Berlin: Walter de Gruyter.

Sternberg, R. (1987). Questions and answers about the nature and teaching of thinking skills. In J. Baron and R. J. Sternberg (Eds.), *Teaching thinking skills: Theory and practice* (pp. 251–259). New York: Freeman.

Swales, J. (1987). Utilizing the literatures in teaching the research paper. *TESOL Quarterly* 17: 575–593.

Swales, J. (1990). *Genre analysis: English in academic and research settings.* New York: Cambridge University Press.

Swales, J. (1998). *Other floors, other voices.* Mahwah, NJ: Lawrence Erlbaum.

TESOL (1997). Guidelines for the certification and preparation of teachers of English to speakers of other languages in the United States. *Directory of professional preparation programs in TESOL in the United States and Canada.* Arlington, VA: TESOL.

TESOL (2000). *ESL standards for pre-K–12 students.* Baltimore, MD: TESOL.

Truscott, J. (1999). The case for "The case against grammar correction in L2 writing classes": A response to Ferris. *Journal of Second Language Writing* 8(2): 111–122.

Vacca, R., Vacca, J., and Bruneu, B. (1997). Teachers reflecting on practice. In J. Flood, S. Brice-Heath, and G. D. Lapp (Eds.), *Handbook of research on teaching literacy through the communicative and visual arts* (pp. 445–450). New York: Simon and Schuster/Macmillan.

Van Maanen, M. (1977). Linking ways of knowing with ways of being practical. *Curriculum Inquiry* 6: 205–228.

Vygotsky, L. S. (1962). *Thought and language.* Cambridge, MA: MIT Press.

Vygotsky, L. S. (1981). The instrumental method in psychology. In J. W. Wertsch (Ed.), *The concept of activity in Soviet psychology* (pp. 147–160). Armonk, NY: Sharpe.

Walton, D. (1993). *Informal logic: A handbook for critical argumentation.* Cambridge: Cambridge University Press.

Wartenberg, T. (1990). *The forms of power: From domination to transformation*. Philadelphia: Temple University Press.

Watson, G., and Glaser, E. M. (1980). *Watson–Glaser critical thinking appraisal*. San Antonio, TX: Psychological Corporation.

Wells, G. (1996). Using the tool-kit of discourse in the activity of teaching and learning. *Mind, Culture, and Activity* 3(2): 74–101.

Wells, G. (1999). *Dialogic inquiry*. New York: Cambridge University Press.

Wertsch, J. (1991). A sociocultural approach to socially shared cognition. In L. Resnick, J. Levine, and S. Teasley (Eds.), *Perspectives on socially shared cognition* (pp. 85–100). Washington, D.C.: American Psychological Association.

Williams, R. (1976). Base and superstructure in Marxist cultural theory. In R. Dale (Ed.), *Schooling and capitalism: A sociological reader*. London: Routledge and Kegan Paul.

Williams, R. (1977). *Marxism and literature*. Oxford: Oxford University Press.

Winocur, S. L. (1985). Project IMPACT. In A. L. Costa (Ed.), *Developing minds* (pp. 210–211). Alexandria, VA: Association for Supervision and Curriculum Development.

Woods, D. (1989). Studying ESL teachers' decision-making: Rationale, methodological issues, and initial results. *Carleton Papers in Applied Linguistics Studies* 6: 107–123.

Woods, J. (1996). *Teacher cognition in language teaching*. New York: Cambridge University Press.

Yates, J., and Orlikowski, W. (1992). Genres of organizational communication: A structural approach to studying communication and media. *Academy of Management Review* 17(2): 299–326.

Yeatman, A. (1994). *Postmodern revisionings of the political*. New York: Routledge.

Yoshikawa, M. (1978). Some Japanese and American cultural characteristics. In M. H. Prosser (Ed.), *The cultural dialogue: An introduction to intercultural communication* (pp. 220–230). Boston: Houghton Mifflin.

Young, R. (1994). Impediments to change in writing-across-the-curriculum programs. In W. R. Winterowd and V. Gillespie (Eds.), *Composition in context: Essays in honor of Donald C. Stewart* (pp. 126–138). Carbondale: Southern Illinois University Press.

Zamel, V. (1983). The composing processes of advanced ESL students: Six case studies. *TESOL Quarterly* 17: 165–187.

Zamel, V. (1984). The author responds. *TESOL Quarterly* 18: 154–157.

Index